YOUR PRESENCE IS A GIFT: CLAIM IT

Written by: Jacques Chambers

Table of Contents

Introduction Of The Book "Your Presence Is A Gift: Claim It"

The true meaning of the gift of presence extends far beyond simply being physically present. We've all experienced moments when we were "there" in body but not in mind, distracted by thoughts or preoccupations. Genuine presence involves a deep mental and emotional investment in the current moment. It means immersing yourself fully in your surroundings – noticing the temperature, the sounds, the scents, and the sights. It also means actively engaging with the people around you or your activity rather than being distracted by screens or other diversions.

Your presence is a profound gift, as the present moment is the only reality you truly have. The future is uncertain and yet to unfold, while the past exists only as a collection of memories colored by emotions. Living in the past or worrying about the future can rob you of the richness of the now. By embracing the gift of presence, you allow yourself to truly experience life rather than merely reflecting on it in hindsight.

This aligns beautifully with the concept of "Presence Is a Gift: Claim It." Claiming your presence means consciously choosing to engage with life in its fullness, acknowledging the value of the present moment. It's about stepping into your life wholeheartedly, leaving distractions and worries behind to savor the gift of now. This practice enriches your experience and deepens your connections with others, making your presence an irreplaceable gift to those around you.

The concept of personal presence as a divine gift.

The concept of personal presence in the Bible is deeply rooted in the idea that it is a divine gift—a spiritual endowment from God that enables individuals to fulfill their unique purpose and influence others in alignment with His will. This presence goes beyond physical attributes or human charisma; it reflects a profound connection with God, empowering individuals to lead, inspire, and enact change in ways that transcend natural abilities.

Personal Presence as a Divine Gift in Biblical Examples

Moses: Moses' transformation from a reluctant leader to a powerful figure demonstrates personal presence as a divine gift. His radiant face after speaking with God (Exodus 34:29-30) manifested this divine endowment. Moses' presence, rooted in his spiritual encounters, carried God's authority and became a tool through which he guided the Israelites. His ability to stand before Pharaoh and lead a nation was not of his own making but a gift from God, equipping him for his extraordinary mission.

David: David's presence exemplifies how God equips individuals with qualities beyond natural talent. While 1 Samuel 16:18 highlights David's bravery, eloquence, and appearance, the statement, "The LORD is with him," underscores his presence as a divine gift. This spiritual empowerment enabled David to defeat

Goliath, lead Israel as a king, and compose Psalms that continue to inspire believers. His influence was a testament to God's gifting, which shaped him into a leader after God's heart (Acts 13:22).

Esther: Esther's rise from obscurity to queen of Persia illustrates how personal presence can be divinely orchestrated for a greater purpose. Her position and influence were not coincidental but part of God's plan, as seen in Esther 4:14: "And who knows if perhaps you have come to the kingdom for such a time as this?" Esther's courage and wisdom were gifts from God, enabling her to act decisively to save her people. Her story reflects how divine gifting positions individuals to fulfill critical roles in God's plan.

Paul: Though outwardly unimpressive, the apostle Paul's presence was profoundly impactful (2 Corinthians 10:10) due to his spiritual authority and unwavering conviction. His ability to establish churches, write transformative epistles, and endure persecution was a divine gift that empowered him for his mission. Paul's presence emanated from his faith and God-given resilience, allowing him to influence countless lives and spread the Gospel across diverse regions.

Divine Gifting and Its Impact

These examples portray personal presence as a divine gift uniquely tailored to the individual's calling. Moses' authority, David's leadership, Esther's courage, and Paul's conviction reflect God's empowerment, enabling them to transcend human limitations. This underscores that personal presence in the biblical sense is not about self-reliance but about allowing God's power to work through individuals, making their influence enduring and impactful.

Thus, the concept of personal presence as a divine gift reminds believers that their ability to lead and influence others is not solely their own but a reflection of God's work within them. By cultivating a close relationship with God and aligning with His purpose, individuals can fully embrace this gift, using it to inspire, guide, and fulfill their divine calling.

The importance of claiming one's dreams and aspirations.

Dreams and ambitions are profound forces shaping your life and career trajectory. They kindle hope, fuel motivation, and provide a bright future roadmap. Recognizing the significance of claiming your dreams and aspirations while understanding their interconnectedness empowers you to set meaningful goals and work diligently to achieve them.

Dreams represent your deepest desires and longings, offering a vision of what you aspire to accomplish or become. They allow you to imagine a life beyond your current circumstances, serving as a beacon of possibility. However, while inspiring, dreams often remain abstract until you claim them and take actionable steps toward their realization.

Ambitions, on the other hand, are the driving force that transforms dreams into reality. They are rooted in effort, persistence, and planning. While dreams may offer a sense of wonder and inspiration, ambitions channel that energy into focused action, ensuring progress and tangible outcomes.

The Importance of Claiming Dreams and Aspirations

Owning your dreams and ambitions is essential to leading a fulfilling and purposeful life. By embracing them fully, you empower yourself to pursue personal growth and overcome obstacles. Here's why claiming your dreams and aspirations matters:

Personal Development

Owning your dreams drives you to improve continuously. It motivates you to enhance your skills, expand your knowledge, and gain valuable experiences, fostering growth and self-improvement.

Career Advancement

Ambitions propel you to take intentional steps in your professional journey, inspiring you to seek opportunities, aim for leadership roles, and excel in your chosen field.

Life Satisfaction

Pursuing and achieving your dreams brings a profound sense of fulfillment, enriching your life with purpose and meaning.

Resilience and Perseverance

Claiming your aspirations helps you build the resilience to navigate challenges and setbacks. It cultivates a determined mindset that keeps you moving forward, even in adversity.

Inspiration to Others

By boldly pursuing your dreams, you inspire those around you, fostering a supportive community of individuals striving to achieve their ambitions.

Striking the Balance

Nurturing dreams and ambitions are vital to unlocking your potential. Allow your dreams to inspire and evolve while using your ambitions to guide your efforts with purpose and direction. By striking a balance between envisioning possibilities and taking actionable steps, you can transform your aspirations into reality.

Claiming your dreams and ambitions is a powerful step toward self-discovery and personal fulfillment. By taking ownership of your aspirations and embracing the journey with focus and determination, you can overcome challenges, achieve meaningful goals, and inspire others to do the same. Unlock your potential by daring to dream boldly and working passionately toward turning those dreams into reality.

Overview Of Spiritual Principles

A Foundation for a Meaningful Life

Spiritual principles are universal truths that guide human behavior and actions, much like the law of gravity governs physical phenomena. For example, when you drop a stone, it falls to the ground—an outcome dictated by natural law. Similarly, consistent honesty fosters trust, illustrating how predictable principles govern human interactions. Life, however, is filled with stressors that can make it feel not very sensible. Applying spiritual principles is essential to navigate these challenges and cultivate a fulfilling existence. Below are nine key spiritual principles and their transformative potential.

Patience and Tolerance

Patience and tolerance are interconnected virtues. Tolerance involves accepting and allowing the existence of perspectives or behaviors you might not agree with. Intolerance often manifests as rigid opinions or actions that harm societal harmony. Cultivating tolerance means seeing the world through others' eyes, reducing harsh judgments, and fostering mutual respect. As tolerance grows, so does patience, enabling a deeper understanding of life's complexities.

Acceptance

Acceptance is about embracing life's realities without necessarily approving of them. It involves acknowledging circumstances beyond your control and finding peace in letting go of resistance. This principle is closely linked to the Serenity Prayer, which emphasizes discernment between what can and cannot be changed. Practicing acceptance reduces frustration, fosters inner peace, and promotes a positive outlook that can influence others.

Open-Mindedness

Open-mindedness entails being receptive to new ideas, perspectives, and possibilities. It allows for thoughtful consideration of differing viewpoints before forming judgments. This principle fosters personal growth, discovery, and honest living. Many struggle to admit a closed mindset, yet embracing open-mindedness can lead to more meaningful relationships and deeper self-awareness.

Gratitude

Gratitude involves appreciating what you have rather than focusing on what you lack. By recognizing the abundance in your life—such as health, relationships, and basic needs—you can shift your perspective from dissatisfaction to contentment. Gratitude diminishes attachment to unfulfilled desires and magnifies the value of present blessings, fostering a sense of fulfillment and reducing the pursuit of the unattainable.

Hope and Faith

Hope and faith are pillars of resilience, offering strength during life's most challenging times. Hope fuels ambition and inspires positive change, while faith replaces fear with courage. These principles create a foundation for envisioning a brighter future and overcoming obstacles. Facing fears with faith enables personal transformation and nurtures optimism, making seemingly impossible goals achievable.

Forgiveness

Forgiveness is one of the most powerful yet misunderstood spiritual principles. It is not about condoning wrongdoing but about freeing yourself from resentment. Holding onto anger or seeking vengeance only prolongs suffering and ties you to negative experiences. Forgiveness allows you to redirect energy towards meaningful pursuits, fostering emotional liberation and inner peace.

Honesty

Honesty begins with being truthful to yourself and extends to others. Expressing your true thoughts and feelings requires courage while maintaining respect and empathy. Practicing honesty reduces manipulation and fosters trust. While it may sometimes be blunt or direct, honesty can be conveyed with kindness, enhancing relationships and self-respect.

Humility

Humility is about embracing your true self without the need for superiority. It involves acknowledging your strengths and limitations while remaining grounded. Humility fosters self-awareness and strengthens relationships by reducing the urge to compare or compete. Those who embody humility exude quiet confidence and are better equipped to navigate life's challenges.

Intention

Living with intention aligns your thoughts, actions, and goals with your deeper purpose. This principle emphasizes mindful decision-making and focuses your efforts on achieving meaningful objectives. For example, someone intending to build wealth might cultivate discipline, work ethic, and financial literacy. Believing in the power of intention allows you to see life's events as interconnected, with each step leading toward your aspirations.

Integrating these nine spiritual principles—patience, tolerance, acceptance, open-mindedness, gratitude, hope, faith, forgiveness, honesty, humility, and intention—can help you create a life rich with meaning and fulfillment. These principles act as a compass, helping you navigate life's stressors while fostering personal growth, inner peace, and harmonious relationships.

The Bible offers profound lessons for individuals pursuing their dreams, emphasizing submission to God's will, humility, perseverance, and the importance of staying focused on the divine path. Examining the lives of King Saul, David, and other biblical figures, we can draw parallels between their journeys and our own, understanding how scriptural principles can guide us toward fulfilling our aspirations while remaining faithful to God's purpose.

1. Seek Divine Wisdom

"Fear of the Lord is the beginning of wisdom" (Proverbs 9:10 NIV).

Saul's Victories marked Saul's early reign because he submitted to God's guidance. However, when he strayed, jealousy and selfishness clouded his judgment, leading to his downfall. In contrast, David sought God's wisdom before engaging in battles, demonstrating that seeking divine direction is crucial for success. For those pursuing dreams, this principle teaches the importance of aligning ambitions with God's wisdom through prayer, Scripture, and reliance on the Holy Spirit. Moses also exemplifies this; his humility and dependence on God's guidance enabled him to lead Israel through extraordinary challenges. Success often begins with acknowledging our limitations and seeking strength from a higher power.

2. Avoid Foolish and Ignorant Disputes

"Don't have anything to do with foolish and stupid arguments, because you know they produce quarrels" (2 Timothy 2:23).

Debating pointless matters can detract from our focus and delay progress toward our dreams. Despite opposition, Nehemiah's steadfast dedication to rebuilding Jerusalem's walls teaches us the value of avoiding distractions. Like Nehemiah, we must maintain clarity and prevent divisive conversations that derail our purpose. Success in achieving our dreams often requires silence in the face of criticism, trusting that God will vindicate us.

3. Be Willing to Accept Advice

"The things which you learned and received and heard and saw in me, these do, and the God of peace will be with you" (Philippians 4:9).

Humility in accepting guidance is pivotal for growth. Timothy thrived as a leader by heeding Paul's mentorship. In contrast, Saul's refusal to fully obey Samuel's instructions cost him his throne. For individuals pursuing their dreams, this principle underlines the necessity of learning from those who have walked similar paths. Constructive feedback, even when difficult to accept, can shape us into better leaders and achievers.

4. Stay Focused on the Goal

"Not that I have already obtained all this, or have already arrived at my goal, but I press on..." (Philippians 3:12).

A divided mind leads to instability (James 1:5-8). Jesus exemplified unwavering focus on God's plan, even as He faced crucifixion, knowing the redemption of humanity was the goal (Hebrews 12:2). Likewise, those pursuing their dreams must remain steadfast, even in adversity. Distractions and setbacks will arise, but maintaining a clear vision of God's purpose allows for perseverance through challenges.

5. Stay Out of Regret

"Forget the former things; do not dwell on the past. See, I am doing a new thing!" (Isaiah 43:18-19).

Regret over past failures can hinder progress. Like David, who repented and moved forward after sinning, we are called to embrace God's grace and focus on the new opportunities He provides. Dreams cannot flourish when weighed down by guilt. Instead, relying on God's mercy allows us to rebuild and restore what was lost, as promised in Joel 2:25.

6. Remember Where Success Comes From

"When you eat and are satisfied... do not forget the Lord your God" (Deuteronomy 11:14).

Biblical history, from the Israelites' idolatry to Solomon's alliances, reveals the dangers of forgetting God amid prosperity. Acknowledging that all success is a gift from God ensures we remain humble and grounded. Zacchaeus, who repented and restored what he wrongfully gained, exemplifies this principle. Unlike the rich young ruler who clung to his wealth, Zacchaeus achieved spiritual fulfillment by prioritizing God over material possessions.

Application to Claiming Dreams

Biblical teachings provide a blueprint for achieving dreams in alignment with God's will. These principles emphasize humility, reliance on divine wisdom, focus, and the ability to grow through repentance and advice. By seeking God's guidance, avoiding distractions, accepting mentorship, and staying grounded in faith, individuals can pursue their dreams with confidence that their path aligns with divine purpose. Following these principles ensures success is achieved and sustained through God's blessing.

Chapter One
Understanding Your Gift

Understanding your gift is a journey of self-discovery, empowerment, and responsibility. It starts with a sense of curiosity and the willingness to explore what sets you apart — those unique abilities, talents, or qualities that feel natural to you and seem to resonate deeply with others. Often, these gifts manifest in areas where you find both ease and passion, whether in creative expression, problem-solving, connecting with people, or inspiring others.

Reflection is key to truly understanding your gift. Pay attention to moments when you feel most alive, purposeful, and aligned. Consider the feedback you receive from others—what they see as your strengths might illuminate aspects of yourself that you overlook or take for granted. Journaling, meditating, or engaging in deep conversations can help clarify this understanding.

Recognizing your gift also means realizing that it's not just about personal fulfillment; it's about how you use it to contribute to the world around you. A gift is most meaningful when shared when it uplifts or adds value to others. This can be in big, bold ways or in quiet, subtle moments—the impact is still profound.

Finally, understanding your gift requires humility and growth. It's about embracing your potential while acknowledging that your gift, like a muscle, needs nurturing, practice, and refinement. Challenges along the way aren't signs of failure but opportunities to grow stronger and more aligned with your purpose.

When you lean into your gift, you step into the flow of life, creating a ripple effect of positivity and meaning for yourself and those around you.

The Gift Within

Each of us carries a unique gift, a potential waiting to be realized. Yet, many of us ignore this inherent treasure. Why does this happen? It often stems from fear — fear of failure or, surprisingly, fear of success. These fears can lead us to avoid the responsibilities or expectations of embracing our gifts. However, neglecting this gift comes at a cost. Left uncared for, it risks being wasted, lost, or overlooked, much like a missed opportunity that could have shaped your life for the better.

As the saying goes, "To whom much is given, much is required." This principle applies universally — to your talents, goals, relationships, and even the future of those you influence, such as your children. Our gifts must be nurtured with care, like seeds requiring water and attention to grow. Without this effort, fulfillment becomes elusive, and life is left devoid of authenticity, filled instead with "Genetically Modified Opinions" — unhealthy, distorted beliefs about us, often shaped by the expectations or judgments of others.

The key to unlocking the potential of this gift lies in our perception. Your life, your circumstances, and your resources are uniquely yours. Comparing yourself to others diminishes the joy of what you already possess. Ask yourself: Are you managing your gifts wisely? Are you disciplined in nurturing your talents, aspirations, and relationships, or do you take them for granted and divert your energy toward unworthy pursuits?

When you care for and cultivate your gifts, you'll often find that they grow and multiply effortlessly. It's as though life expands your capacity to contribute, aligning you with what the world needs. Conversely, negligence or ingratitude can lead to a shift where these blessings are diminished or even removed, not out of malice but to protect you from harm or redirect you to a better path.

The gift within is resilient. Like seeds, we must sometimes be repotted — moved out of our comfort zones to thrive in new environments. Feeling apprehensive about such transitions is natural, but growth often requires discomfort. Don't stifle your potential out of fear or a desire to fit in. Embrace your gift, nurture it with intention, and trust that, no matter where life takes you, your roots will grow deeper, and your branches will stretch farther, offering the fruit of your true purpose to the world.

"Human presence" is a spiritual and personal asset, embodying a deep connection to ourselves and others. It reflects the essence of being truly present, offering a sense of authenticity that nurtures meaningful relationships and inner growth.

This presence goes beyond mere physicality; it is the ability to engage fully in the moment, to listen with empathy, and to respond with intention. Spiritually, it anchors us to a higher sense of purpose and interconnectedness, allowing us to align with values that transcend the material world. It enhances our ability to build trust, foster compassion, and create a positive impact on those around us.

By cultivating human presence, we unlock the potential to navigate life with clarity and resilience. It encourages self-awareness, helping us understand our emotions and actions while remaining open to growth. In a world that often demands speed and multitasking, embracing the depth of presence reminds us to slow down, honor our experiences, and truly connect with what it means to be human.

How divine creation endows everyone with unique qualities.

The concept of humanity being created in the image of God, known in theological terms as Imago Dei, carries profound implications for understanding human nature and purpose. This idea asserts that humans intrinsically reflect divine qualities, not merely in physical form but across moral, spiritual, and intellectual dimensions. Attributes such as rationality, creativity, and the capacity for relationship mirror the divine nature and highlight humanity's unique standing within creation.

Divine Creation and Unique Qualities

Genesis 1:27 declares, "So God created man in His own image; in the image of God, He created him; male and female He created them." This foundational verse emphasizes that being made in God's image imbues humanity with inherent dignity and exceptional qualities. These qualities include rationality—the ability to think and reason; morality—a sense of right and wrong; and relationality—the capacity to form deep, meaningful connections. These traits set humans apart from the rest of creation and underline a divine purpose: to steward the earth and live communion with God.

The uniqueness of human nature as a reflection of the divine establishes a moral framework that upholds equality and dignity. Recognizing the Imago Dei in every individual creates a moral imperative to treat others with respect and compassion, affirming the sanctity of life regardless of race, gender, or status. This theological truth has historically inspired social justice and human rights movements, offering a foundation for ethical behavior rooted in acknowledging divine likeness in all people.

Despite this noble beginning, human nature was profoundly altered by the fall. Genesis 3 recounts the disobedience of Adam and Eve, introducing sin into the world and disrupting the harmony of divine creation. This act led to separation from God, and as Romans 5:12 explains, "Sin entered the world through one man and death through sin." This fallen nature is characterized by a struggle between the desire to reflect divine qualities and the propensity toward sin.

The Apostle Paul vividly describes this internal conflict in Romans 7:18-19: "For I have the desire to do what is good, but I cannot carry it out. For I do not do the good I want to do, but the evil I do not want to do—this I keep on doing." This duality reflects the tension between humanity's divine design and its corrupted state, a theme woven throughout Scripture and evident in daily human experience.

Redemption and Renewal Through Christ

The New Testament provides hope for overcoming this fallen nature through the redemptive work of Christ. As 2 Corinthians 5:17 proclaims, "If anyone is in Christ, he is a new creation. The old has passed away; behold, the new has come." Through faith in Jesus, believers are empowered to live in alignment with God's original design, reflecting divine qualities more fully. This transformation, facilitated by the Holy Spirit, allows cultivating virtues embodying the Imago Dei, such as love, patience, and self-control.

The Role of the Holy Spirit in Restoration

The Holy Spirit is instrumental in restoring and aligning human nature with its divine purpose. Galatians 5:16-17 teaches, "Walk by the Spirit, and you will not gratify the desires of the flesh. For the flesh desires what is contrary to the Spirit, and the Spirit what is contrary to the flesh." The Spirit empowers believers to bear the fruit of righteousness, enabling them to live out their divine calling and reflect God's image in their actions and relationships.

Glorification: The Fulfillment of Divine Design

Ultimately, Scripture points to a future glorification where human nature will be fully restored to reflect God's perfection. Philippians 3:21 promises, "He will transform our lowly bodies so that they will be like His glorious body." This eschatological hope underscores the completion of God's creative work, where human nature will no longer be marred by sin but fully embody the Imago Dei, exemplifying divine qualities in their purest form.

The Relationship Between Divine Creation and Human Qualities

The divine act of creating humans in His image endows them with unique qualities that underpin moral responsibility, relational depth, and creative capacity. These attributes are not only reflections of God's nature but also tools for fulfilling His purpose. The ability to reason, make ethical decisions, and form communities mirrors God's wisdom, holiness, and relationality, calling humanity to live in harmony with each other and creation. The ongoing journey of redemption and ultimate glorification reveals God's intention to restore these qualities fully, reaffirming humanity's role as the pinnacle of His creation.

This divine image endows humans with unique attributes such as rationality, morality, creativity, and the capacity for a relationship with God. Human uniqueness is further emphasized through the mandate of dominion and stewardship over creation.

The Divine Blueprint

A Divine Blueprint can be envisioned as a comprehensive guide to your soul's purpose and path, crafted before your incarnation. It represents the intricate design of your destiny, encompassing your life's purpose while transcending it. This blueprint serves as a template to align with your higher self, guiding you to embody your authentic essence and fulfill the mission you are meant to undertake in this lifetime. It is both a roadmap for being true to your inner self and a guide for expressing your higher self in the physical realm.

The Divine Blueprint harmonizes two key aspects of existence: being and doing. On one hand, it emphasizes the importance of embodying your true self and embracing your authentic nature without external pretenses. Conversely, it calls for purposeful action—seeking, discovering, and actualizing your life's purpose. This duality balances the feminine essence of introspection and authenticity and the masculine drive toward action and achievement.

How Does the Divine Blueprint Relate to Life Purpose?

Your purpose in life is intricately woven into your Divine Blueprint. Your path is filled with intuitive nudges or callings, guiding you toward your higher purpose. These callings are moments of inner clarity that urge you to act, often leading to significant personal growth or realizing your unique contributions to the world. They may begin as subtle signals—a spark of curiosity or a sense of direction—and gradually evolve into significant milestones that steer you closer to your soul's destiny.

The Divine Blueprint recognizes that these callings are not static; they shift and transform throughout life, adapting to your growth and experiences. Small, deliberate steps can pave the way toward profound achievements, while bold leaps may signal pivotal moments in your journey. Regardless of the scale, these actions align with the higher vision of your blueprint, ensuring you remain aligned with your soul's purpose.

Understanding and embracing your Divine Blueprint allows you to navigate life with a sense of purpose and clarity. It reminds you that your existence is not just about achieving goals but about expressing your higher self and maintaining harmony between your authentic being and purposeful doing.

The idea of a preordained purpose (Jeremiah 29:11).

Embarking on the journey of understanding God's purpose for your life can evoke excitement and uncertainty. It's comforting to know that the Bible offers assurance in Jeremiah 29:11, a verse that serves as a divine promise: "For I know the plans I have for you," declares the Lord, "plans to prosper you and not to harm you, plans to give you hope and a future." This verse is a powerful reminder of a preordained purpose—a divine blueprint crafted uniquely for everyone, full of hope and promise.

Understanding the Historical Context

To appreciate the depth of Jeremiah 29:11, it's essential to consider its historical backdrop. The prophet Jeremiah spoke these words to the Israelites during their exile in Babylon, a time of displacement, despair, and uncertainty. In this turbulent period, God's message provided a beacon of hope, assuring them that their suffering was not the end but a part of a greater plan for restoration and prosperity.

In our modern lives, we, too, face seasons of struggle that leave us questioning the purpose of our trials. Yet Jeremiah 29:11 reassures us that even in these moments, God's preordained plan is unfolding—a plan not to harm but to bring growth, fulfillment, and a future filled with His blessings.

Aligning with God's Plan

Discovering and aligning with God's preordained purpose often begins with seeking His guidance through prayer, meditation, and Scripture. In quiet moments of reflection, we open ourselves to divine whispers that guide our steps. Through studying His word, we gain clarity on His promises, a foundation for trust and obedience.

This alignment also requires faith in God's timing. The fast-paced world often tempts us to prioritize quick success and material gains. Still, God's plan invites us to detach from worldly pressures and embrace a purpose rooted in spiritual fulfillment. Making countercultural choices—valuing relationships over accomplishments or choosing service over self-interest—reflects a life aligned with His divine will.

Trusting the Process

Trusting God's process involves surrendering personal timelines and embracing His divine schedule. While setbacks and delays may feel like obstacles, they are integral to the growth and preparation required to fulfill His purpose. These moments challenge us to develop patience, resilience, and unwavering faith, transforming trials into steppingstones.

Viewing Challenges Through the Lens of Purpose

The challenges we encounter often serve as refining tools in God's grand design. Rather than seeing obstacles as deterrents, we can view them as opportunities for growth. These experiences shape us, equipping us with the strength, empathy, and perspective to fulfill our divine calling.

Celebrating Small Victories

Each step forward, no matter how small, reflects progress in fulfilling God's purpose. These victories, whether spiritual breakthroughs or acts of kindness, remind us that God's preordained plan unfolds daily. Celebrating these moments cultivates gratitude, shifts focus from immediate challenges and reinforces our faith in His promises.

A Journey of Continual Growth

Understanding God's purpose is not a one-time revelation but a lifelong journey of spiritual growth. We become more attuned to His guidance as we deepen our relationship with God through prayer, worship, and community. This ongoing process strengthens our faith, helping us remain steadfast in His promises.

Encouraging Others in Their Purpose

Living out God's purpose involves inspiring and supporting others on their journeys. Sharing experiences, insights, and faith creates a ripple effect of encouragement and hope. This act of service aligns with God's design, enriching not only others but also deepening our understanding of His plan.

Surrendering to the Divine Will

At the heart of embracing God's purpose lies surrender. It is an act of trust—relinquishing personal desires and fears to align fully with His higher plans. Surrendering doesn't signify giving up but giving over, acknowledging that his preordained purpose is perfect and His timing impeccable.

Living Jeremiah 29:11 Daily

The assurance of Jeremiah 29:11 invites us to live with open hearts, trusting in God's preordained purpose. It calls us to view our lives as part of a divine narrative, where every moment—joyful or challenging—contributes to a greater story of hope and fulfillment. By embracing this perspective, we can find peace, purpose, and gratitude in the present, confident in God's planned future.

Examples of individuals in the Bible who lived their purpose.

In today's fast-paced world, living without much thought or intention is easy. However, many figures in the Bible exemplified lives filled with purpose and conscious direction. For those seeking inspiration for intentional living, the Bible offers remarkable examples.

Key Biblical Figures of Intentional Living

Notable individuals such as Daniel, Ruth, Esther, Paul, and Jesus demonstrated intentionality by making deliberate choices to follow God's calling, even amid uncertainty and adversity. This guide explores their stories and the purposeful decisions that shaped their lives. By reflecting on their examples, we can gain wisdom and motivation to live our faith more intentionally.

Daniel's Commitment to Prayer

Unwavering Devotion

Daniel exemplified steadfastness in prayer, maintaining his daily practice of praying three times, even when facing persecution. His habit of prayer was deeply rooted long before trials emerged, showcasing his profound dependency on and love for God. When a decree forbade prayer, Daniel continued his practice without hesitation (Daniel 6:10), risking his life to uphold his faith. This unyielding commitment inspires us to prioritize our relationship with God over external pressures.

Uncompromising Faith

Daniel refused to compromise his beliefs, boldly continuing his prayers despite the king's decree. His actions reflect his integrity and prioritization of spiritual conviction over personal safety. Daniel's example challenges us to evaluate our faith, urging us to stand firm in our convictions regardless of external threats.

Ruth's Loyalty and Service

Choosing to Follow Naomi

Ruth's loyalty shone when she chose to stay with her mother-in-law Naomi after losing their husbands. Despite Naomi urging her to remain in Moab, Ruth vowed unwavering support, saying, "Where you go, I will go; your people will be my people and your God my God" (Ruth 1:16). This selfless act underscores Ruth's deep commitment and courage in leaving her homeland to embrace a new life.

Selfless Service

Ruth worked tirelessly to provide for Naomi, humbly gathering grain in the fields and earning the favor of Boaz, a relative of Naomi's late husband. Her humility and dedication led to her inclusion in Jesus' genealogy, an extraordinary testament to her faith and service. Ruth's story encourages us to live purposefully through acts of loyalty and kindness.

Esther's Courage and Boldness

Risking Her Life for Justice

As queen, Esther courageously intervened to save her people, the Jews, from annihilation. Despite the law prohibiting her from approaching the king uninvited, Esther declared, "If I perish, I perish" (Esther 4:16). Her bravery highlights the importance of prioritizing justice over personal safety.

Speaking Against Injustice

Esther boldly confronted King Xerxes, exposing Haman's plot against the Jews. Her willingness to speak truth to power reversed the deadly decree and Haman's downfall. Esther's actions remind us of the power of advocacy and the need to stand against injustice, regardless of the risks involved.

Paul's Wholehearted Obedience

A Radical Transformation

Paul's life dramatically changed after encountering Jesus on the road to Damascus (Acts 9:1-9). Once a persecutor of Christians, Paul became a passionate advocate for the Gospel. His transformation underscores God's ability to redirect lives for divine purposes.

Relentless Evangelism

Paul tirelessly spread the Gospel across the Roman Empire, enduring hardships to fulfill his mission. His letters reflect his deep commitment, as in statements like, "To live is Christ and to die is gain" (Philippians 1:21). Paul's perseverance inspires us to live with unwavering devotion to God's calling.

Jesus' Complete Surrender to the Father's Will

Focused on His Purpose

Jesus lived with a clear mission: to serve and give His life as a ransom for many (Mark 10:45). From His youth, He prioritized His Father's work, demonstrating unwavering focus even in the face of distractions or opposition (Luke 2:49).

Courage and Clarity

Jesus confronted religious hypocrisy, upheld truth, and maintained His mission despite challenges. His prayerful reliance on the Father exemplifies a life of complete surrender. Even in His final moments, Jesus' commitment to His purpose remained resolute.

These biblical figures remind us of the power of living with intention. Their stories encourage us to embrace purpose, faith, and boldness, demonstrating that intentionality can lead to profound spiritual growth and impact.

Recognizing Your Worth

Every individual is born with an inherent sense of worth. It is not something that must be earned or validated by external achievements. Unfortunately, many of us fail to recognize this intrinsic value, often believing we must attain certain milestones or levels of success before deeming ourselves worthy. This mindset, however, is far from the truth. You are worthy just as you are, and acknowledging this fundamental truth is the first step toward embracing self-worth. When we recognize our value, we pave the way for self-acceptance, self-love, and a more fulfilling and joyful life.

The Importance of Self-Worth

Self-worth forms the foundation of a healthy self-esteem and identity. It is the cornerstone of self-acceptance and self-love, both critical for feeling deserving of love and acceptance from others. Without this solid foundation, individuals may grapple with feelings of inadequacy, making building and maintaining positive relationships challenging.

The absence of self-worth often leads to negative consequences. People with limited self-worth may engage in toxic relationships or self-defeating behaviors, such as negative self-talk, avoidance of intimacy, and chronic comparisons to others. These behaviors reinforce feelings of inadequacy and unworthiness, creating a cycle that can be difficult to break. For those who have experienced abusive or unhealthy relationships, this cycle is even more pronounced, as self-doubt and shame often keep them trapped in harmful situations.

The Roots of Low Self-Worth

A lack of self-worth is frequently rooted in early life experiences. Adults who endured childhood neglect or abuse often struggle with insecure attachments and challenges in forming a healthy sense of self-worth. Attachment styles such as anxious-ambivalent, avoidant, or dismissive can increase vulnerability to issues like depression, anxiety, and repeated patterns of unhealthy relationships. Similarly, individuals raised in environments where their skills and competencies were not acknowledged may carry feelings of worthlessness and low self-esteem into adulthood.

How to Recognize and Cultivate Your Worth

Reconnecting with your inherent worth is a transformative journey that requires intentional effort and self-compassion. Here are five practical ways to begin:

Acknowledge Your Accomplishments

Reflect on your achievements, no matter how small they may seem. Please make a list of these accomplishments and revisit them when self-doubt arises. Recognizing your capabilities helps reinforce your sense of self-worth.

Surround Yourself with Positive Influences

The company you keep plays a significant role in shaping your self-esteem. Spend time with people who uplift and support you, and distance yourself from those who bring negativity. Positive relationships foster a greater sense of value and belonging.

Practice Self-Compassion

Treat yourself with kindness, especially when you make mistakes. Acknowledge your efforts and successes, no matter how modest. Understanding that you deserve compassion is crucial for building self-worth.

Contribute to Others

Acts of kindness and service remind us of our ability to impact the world positively. Helping others reinforces the idea that you are valuable and can make a difference.

Prioritize Self-Care

Taking care of your physical and mental well-being is essential for fostering self-worth. Regular exercise, healthy eating, sufficient rest, and dedicating time to activities you enjoy all contribute to feeling good about yourself.

Relating Self-Worth to Recognizing Your Worth

Recognizing your worth is not just about understanding your value—it's about internalizing it and allowing it to shape your actions and mindset. By acknowledging your accomplishments, seeking positive relationships, and practicing self-compassion, you reinforce the belief that you deserve love, respect, and happiness. This recognition forms the foundation for a healthier, more confident sense of self, enabling you to break free from cycles of negativity and embrace a life of fulfillment and joy.

Remember, external measures or others' opinions do not define your worth. It is an intrinsic quality within you, waiting to be recognized and celebrated.

The significance of self-worth in faith and personal growth.

Understanding our self-worth and experiencing personal growth are deeply intertwined in our faith journey. As Christians, we must reflect on God's boundless love for us and how this divine affection shapes our identity. Faith offers a framework for self-discovery, empowering us to recognize our intrinsic value as God's creations. This understanding lays the foundation for meaningful personal growth as we align our lives with the virtues and teachings of faith.

Faith is a powerful ally in pursuing personal development, providing guidance, strength, and perspective. Belief in a higher power or divine plan offers reassurance during life's uncertainties, helping us stay motivated and focused. When anchored in faith, personal growth becomes more than self-improvement—it becomes a journey of spiritual alignment, where every goal is pursued with purpose and clarity.

Through prayer, meditation, and worship, individuals can draw strength to overcome challenges and remain steadfast in their growth journey. Christian teachings on compassion, humility, patience, and forgiveness offer a blueprint for navigating life's complexities with integrity and grace. By embodying these virtues, individuals can foster personal growth while staying true to their faith.

The Scripture, "Practice these things, immerse yourself in them, so that all may see your progress" (1 Timothy 4:15), underscores the value of active engagement in personal and spiritual development. Faith inspires a holistic approach, addressing the intellectual and emotional aspects of growth and the spiritual dimensions. This balanced growth fosters development across mind, body, and Spirit, leading to an enriched and purposeful life.

Faith also transforms how we perceive failure and setbacks. Rather than viewing them as defeats, faith reframes challenges as opportunities for learning and growth. Trusting in God's plan provides resilience and optimism, encouraging us to approach obstacles with hope and determination.

Moving Forward in Growth and Faith

Personal growth is a dynamic, lifelong journey fueled by self-awareness, resilience, and a commitment to learning. Faith is a compass on this journey, offering guidance, strength, and a deeper sense of purpose. Individuals can achieve a fulfilling and value-driven life by aligning personal growth with spiritual principles.

At Pathfinders Pastoral Care Ministries, we encourage individuals to embrace spiritual thinking to guide their growth. Personal development involves more than achieving goals; it is about becoming the best version of oneself through experiences, introspection, and faith.

The Role of Faith in Enhancing Personal Growth

Enhanced Self-Worth through Self-Awareness

Faith teaches us to see ourselves as beloved creations of God, inherently worthy of love and respect. Self-reflection and spiritual practices can help individuals gain insights into their thoughts, emotions, and behaviors. This awareness fosters confidence and clarity, enabling deliberate and value-driven decisions.

Increased Resilience through Faith

Personal growth often requires facing adversity. Faith strengthens resilience by reassuring that no challenge is insurmountable with God's guidance. Trusting in divine support equips individuals to adapt to change, manage stress, and persevere in trials.

Improved Relationships Rooted in Faith

When individuals embrace compassion, humility, and forgiveness, their relationships become more authentic and meaningful. Faith-based growth enables better communication, emotional intelligence, and empathy, fostering mutual respect and deeper connections with others.

Fulfillment Aligned with Faith and Purpose

Faith encourages individuals to align their goals with their core values, creating a profound sense of purpose. When actions resonate with spiritual principles, fulfillment surpasses material success, nurturing a life of joy and contentment.

Continuous Learning with Faith as a Guide

Faith emphasizes lifelong learning as a path to wisdom and growth. Through Scripture, education, or life experiences, individuals expand their knowledge and skills, becoming more capable and versatile. This development enriches both personal and professional aspects of life.

Incorporating faith into personal growth elevates the journey by emphasizing self-worth, resilience, and a deep connection to one's values. By nurturing spiritual and personal dimensions simultaneously, individuals can lead lives that are not only successful but also deeply meaningful.

If you or someone you love is ready to embark on a transformative journey of faith and personal growth, Pathfinders Pastoral Care Ministries offers support and guidance at every step.

The Role of Identity

Your identity forms the foundation of your sense of self, distinguishing you from others with a unique combination of traits. While you may share similarities with others, your identity is exclusively yours, setting you apart. It also provides a sense of continuity, the understanding that you remain the same individual over time, whether reflecting on the person you were two years ago or envisioning who you will be.

Beyond shaping who you are, identity plays a significant role in how you interact with others and navigate the world around you. A robust sense of identity influences your behavior, choices, and relationships, offering clarity and stability in various aspects of life.

The Importance of Identity

A strong sense of identity is pivotal for personal growth and social interaction. It provides several key benefits:

Fostering Self-Awareness

Understanding your identity allows you to explore who you are—your preferences, values, motivations, and relationships. This self-awareness serves as a foundation for personal development.

Providing Direction and Motivation

A clear identity helps align one's actions with one's values and goals. It offers a sense of purpose, enabling one to make decisions and pursue ambitions with confidence and clarity.

Enabling Healthy Relationships

Knowing and accepting yourself fosters meaningful connections with others. It encourages authentic interactions, effective communication, and the establishment and respect of boundaries.

Grounding in Uncertainty

Dr. Qaadir emphasizes that identity serves as an anchor during challenging times. Your sense of self can provide stability and perspective when external circumstances feel chaotic.

Enhancing Decision-Making

A well-defined identity helps you make decisions aligned with your core values and long-term aspirations. It reduces confusion and the pressure to conform, allowing you to navigate choices confidently.

Promoting Community Participation

Identity, shaped by cultural, social, and historical contexts, fosters a sense of pride in your heritage. It encourages active societal participation and the expression of unique perspectives, empowering you to contribute to meaningful change.

In contrast, a weak sense of identity can leave you emotionally adrift during stressful times and uncertain when facing significant life decisions, as noted by Dr. Qaadir.

Strategies for Reflecting on Your Identity

Reflecting on your identity can strengthen your sense of self and deepen your understanding of your place in the world. Dr. Qaadir suggests several methods:

Art: Engaging in creative expression helps process emotions and explore identity in unique, personal ways.

Reading: Narrative stories provide diverse perspectives, encouraging reflection on your values and beliefs.

Journaling: Writing about your experiences, thoughts, and feelings promotes self-awareness and emotional clarity.

Conversation: Discussing ideas with others exposes you to different viewpoints and helps refine your identity.

Nature: Time spent in nature offers solitude and perspective, creating a space for introspection.

Relationships: Surrounding yourself with individuals who share your core values but differ in other aspects of identity enhances learning and broadens your understanding of yourself and others.

How identity shapes aspirations

When reflecting on personal goals and passions, identity is the foundational element that influences the aspirations and ambitions one establishes. Identity encompasses a person's values, beliefs, experiences, and self-perception, all of which shape the lens through which they view the world and determine what is meaningful to them. Goals often serve as a mirror, reflecting an individual's deepest values and priorities, while the passions they choose to pursue provide a sense of purpose and fulfillment rooted in their core identity.

For instance, someone who identifies strongly with a commitment to environmental sustainability may aspire to work in fields that promote ecological preservation, such as renewable energy or conservation. Conversely, individuals whose identity centers around creativity and self-expression may gravitate toward artistic or entrepreneurial endeavors that allow them to manifest their unique perspective.

Identity not only shapes the "what" of aspirations but also the "how" and "why." A person who values resilience and hard work may set ambitious, long-term goals requiring sustained effort. At the same time, someone who identifies with community and collaboration may prioritize goals that involve teamwork or social impact. Even how people respond to challenges is influenced by their identity, as it governs their attitudes toward perseverance, adaptability, and success.

Identity evolves as individuals encounter new experiences and refine their understanding of themselves. This evolution can lead to shifts in aspirations, illustrating how dynamic and interconnected identity and goals are. Ultimately, by understanding and embracing their identity, individuals can set authentic goals that resonate deeply with their true selves, fostering a life rich in purpose and alignment with their inner values.

How can faith shape our view of ourselves

Faith is more than a belief in something greater than ourselves; it is a profound guiding force that touches every aspect of our lives. It shapes our identity, influences our decisions, and transforms how we approach relationships, work, and personal well-being. But how does faith truly impact how we see ourselves? Faith and belief are interconnected yet distinct forces that profoundly influence our self-perception, providing a lens through which we view ourselves and the world around us.

For followers of Yeshua, faith offers more than spiritual guidance—it lays the foundation for living with purpose, integrity, and resilience. Faith acts as a beacon in life's uncertainties, a steady force that supports us when we stumble and elevates us when we strive. It instills a sense of belonging, value, and hope, reminding us that we are part of a greater purpose. These truths shape our self-view, assuring that we are loved, worthy, and capable of overcoming life's challenges.

At its core, faith is about trusting in a reality that extends beyond what is tangible. This unshakeable conviction allows us to see ourselves not as flawed or inadequate but as individuals with inherent value, created for a divine purpose. It encourages acceptance, replacing self-condemnation with understanding and self-compassion. Faith empowers us to trust in our potential and recognize our worth, even when we face setbacks or self-doubt.

The power of belief is equally transformative. Beliefs, silent yet potent, act as the framework for our thoughts and actions. What we believe about ourselves directly impacts our confidence, self-esteem, and the paths we choose. For example, if we think we are unworthy, this mindset may limit our ability to pursue opportunities or maintain fulfilling relationships. However, believing in our strengths and skills can be life-changing, driving us to achieve goals, embrace challenges, and succeed.

Faith and belief together form a powerful duo that shapes our self-perception. Faith assures us that we are part of something greater, loved, and supported by a higher power. It fosters resilience, helping us to navigate life's trials with courage and grace. Belief, on the other hand, aligns our internal narrative with this divine truth. By aligning our beliefs with the principles of faith, we create a self-image rooted in confidence, hope, and purpose.

Moreover, faith encourages us to see ourselves through a lens of divine love and acceptance. It reminds us that our value is not determined by societal standards but by the inherent worth given to us by our Creator. This perspective reshapes how we treat ourselves, encouraging self-care, forgiveness, and growth. Faith and belief work together to transform our relationship with ourselves and how we interact with the world, equipping us to live meaningful and fulfilling lives.

Dreaming with Purpose

Dreams often appear random and difficult to decipher, yet they weave your thoughts and emotions into meaningful patterns. By studying these patterns, you can uncover the awe of God's presence and work in your life. An intentional approach to your dreams can help you find purpose within them. When you consciously use your dreams to achieve specific goals—such as making decisions, solving problems, healing from emotional pain, seeking encouragement, or generating creative ideas—you create a bridge between your waking and sleeping lives. Dreaming with purpose can guide you toward achieving your aspirations.

Have you ever wanted to "sleep on it" for fresh insight? Dreaming about a specific topic can provide divine wisdom and clarity. For instance, while writing Wake Up to Wonder, I regularly asked God for inspiration through my dreams. Time and again, I found my prayers answered. Each morning, I recorded every detail of my dreams, often illuminating the guidance I sought before sleeping.

This intentional process is known as dream incubation. The term originates from the Greek word incubation, meaning to nurture something in a favorable environment for growth. You can use dream incubation to channel your dreams toward specific purposes by following these steps:

Clarify Your Purpose: Decide what you want to dream about and why. Identify a specific issue you hope to understand or resolve, whether making an important decision, seeking healing, finding encouragement, or uncovering creative solutions. Choose one purpose for each dream to maintain focus.

Create a Relaxing Environment: Optimize your bedroom for rest by removing distractions like electronic devices and incorporating relaxing elements such as soothing music or soft blankets. Prepare your mind and body for sleep with calming activities like a warm bath or quiet reflection. Dedicate at least 15 minutes before bedtime to pray and center your thoughts.

Pray with Intention: Reflect on the issue you want to address and pray about it before falling asleep. Speak your prayer aloud to reinforce it in your mind, and consider writing it on a piece of paper to place under your pillow. As you drift to sleep, meditate on your dream's purpose and trust that it will provide insight. Ease into sleep with an open mind and without fear, expecting to gain wisdom from your dreams.

Document Your Dreams: Upon waking, immediately record the details of your dreams in a journal or voice recorder kept by your bedside. These notes will help you reflect on and interpret your dreams, seeking God's guidance in uncovering their meaning.

By purposefully dreaming, you'll notice awe-inspiring patterns that reveal God's guidance and activity in your life. This practice deepens your connection to your dreams and faith, empowering you to find clarity and achieve your goals.

How to identify dreams that align with your values and faith.

Your values are the principles and beliefs guiding your life and work. They shape your priorities and serve as an internal compass, helping you determine if your life aligns with your vision and aspirations. They play a crucial role in decision-making, particularly in challenging situations, and act as a foundation for building meaningful, lasting relationships.

Values also influence your thoughts, words, and actions, ensuring your growth aligns with your authentic self. By anchoring your decisions to your values, you can create a future that reflects your desires and aspirations. For example, if you value environmental stewardship, you may be drawn to work in industries or initiatives that support sustainability rather than those that harm the planet.

The Role of Values in Simplifying Life

When you are clear on your values, they help declutter your life by providing a clear framework for decision-making. They allow you to focus on what truly matters, enabling you to navigate your personal and professional journeys confidently and purposefully.

Gaining Clarity on Your Values

To help you clarify your values, you can use a practical tool like the "Crystal Clear Values" worksheet. This resource includes simple steps, reflective questions, and a comprehensive list of potential values, empowering you to identify the ones that resonate most deeply with you. You can add your own if you don't see a value that fits.

The first step is to identify your top five core values for your personal and professional life. Once you have chosen these, take the time to define each one in your own words—how you perceive and live out these values, rather than relying on societal, familial, or dictionary definitions. If a value applies to personal and professional contexts, consider how its application may differ.

Next, reflect on whether these values are currently evident in your life. Ask yourself:

Are these values guiding my personal decisions?

Are they influencing my professional choices?

If you find gaps, think about the steps you can take to align your life with these values better. This process will naturally lead to further introspection and questions such as:

Where are these values already present?

What changes do I need to make to live in greater alignment with them?

Aligning Your Values with Your Dreams and Faith

As you clarify your values, consider how they intersect with your dreams and faith. Your dreams should reflect your core values, serving as a natural extension of what you hold dear. For instance, if your faith emphasizes compassion and service, your aspirations may involve work or pursuits that benefit others and align with those principles.

Faith often provides a moral and spiritual framework that complements your values, giving additional depth to your dreams. Reflect on questions like:

Do my dreams honor my values and faith?

How can I use my values and faith as a guide to make my dreams a reality?

By aligning your values, faith, and dreams, you create an authentic and purpose-driven life. This alignment ensures your goals resonate deeply and inspire you to take meaningful action toward a fulfilling future.

Recognizing and understanding your core values is essential for creating a life that is not only happier but also healthier. Your values are the guiding principles influencing your decisions and actions, ensuring that your choices align with what satisfies you and connects you to your deeper sense of purpose. Living according to your values creates a more authentic life filled with meaning and fulfillment.

Identifying Your Core Values: Step Process

Step 1: Start with a Beginner's Mind

Approach the process of identifying your values with an open mind. Let go of preconceived notions or old beliefs that might cloud your understanding. Clear your mental slate to make room for discovering what truly matters to you.

Step 2: Create Your List of Personal Values

The key is to discover your values, not just pick them. Reflect on significant moments, deeply held beliefs, and personal rules that guide your behavior. Don't worry about the number of values you identify at this stage; let your list grow freely.

Step 3: Chunk Your Values into Related Groups

Once you have your list, group related values together. For instance, values like responsibility and punctuality fall into one category, while values like learning and growth belong in another. This helps to see patterns in what's important to you.

Step 4: Highlight the Central Theme of Each Value Group

For each group of values, select a word or phrase that captures the essence of that category. For example, if your group includes honesty and transparency, the central theme might be "integrity." This step simplifies your values and makes them easier to understand and live by.

Step 5: Determine Your Top Personal Values

With your groups in mind, narrow your list to the five to ten values that are most important to you. These core values will guide your personal and professional choices and be the foundation of your decisions.

Living in Alignment with Your Core Values

Craft Personal Values Statements

To solidify your connection with each value, write a brief statement for each one. This personal definition clarifies why the value matters to you and reminds you what's truly important in your life.

Test the Ecology of Each Value

Evaluate how each of your core values fits into your life. Ensure they complement each other, forming a balanced and cohesive system of beliefs. This step helps you avoid conflicts between your values and ensures they work harmoniously to guide your decisions.

By engaging in this reflective process and being mindful of how each value impacts your life, you will gain a deeper understanding of yourself and your true priorities. This clarity will help you make decisions that are both intentional and meaningful.

The Benefits of Identifying Your Core Personal Values

Knowing and naming your core values offers numerous benefits, from simplifying decision-making to improving your relationships and overall happiness. When you align your actions with your values, life becomes more purposeful and fulfilling. You'll also find it easier to set and achieve goals that resonate with your true desires, which increases your sense of accomplishment.

Furthermore, understanding your core values strengthens your resilience, helping you navigate difficult situations more easily. When setbacks occur, you can rely on your values to guide you through adversity, enabling you to recover more quickly and remain true to your beliefs.

Benefits of Identifying Core Personal Values

- Enhanced self-understanding
- Simplified decision-making
- More purposeful actions
- Strengthened relationships
- Easier goal-setting
- Healthier boundaries

- Increased resilience
- Greater overall happiness

Uncovering and living by your core values transforms your life, making it more authentic, meaningful, and joyful.

Practical Strategies to Live by Your Values

Setting Healthy Boundaries

When you know your values, it becomes easier to establish boundaries that protect you from outside pressures. These boundaries help you maintain your authenticity and prevent you from being swayed by things that don't align with your true self.

Effective Goal Setting

Understanding your core values can guide you in setting meaningful and achievable goals. Whether you're planning for the near or distant future, aligning your goals with your values makes them more focused and fulfilling.

Improving Relationships

Being clear about your values also enhances your relationships. By understanding your values and respecting those of others, you create a foundation of trust, mutual respect, and authentic connection. This makes it easier to navigate differences and grow together.

Reflecting on Meaningful Life Moments

Reflecting on key moments can reveal which values matter most to you. Significant achievements, challenges, or relationships often highlight your deepest beliefs, helping you understand what drives you.

Paying Attention to Sources of Anger and Dissatisfaction

Times of anger or dissatisfaction can indicate that you're not living in alignment with your values. By examining the underlying causes of these emotions, you can gain insight into what matters most to you. For example, frustration at work may stem from issues like unfairness, lack of control, or insufficient recognition, all of which point to underlying values like fairness, autonomy, and appreciation.

Identifying Your Core Values: A Step-by-Step Guide

This section walks you through the process of identifying your core values. Starting with a beginner's mind and clearing your mental space, you create an open environment for discovering what matters most. Next, you'll compile a list of personal values, group them into themes, and narrow your list to a manageable set of core values.

Through this process, you will gain clarity about yourself and begin to make choices that reflect your deepest beliefs, ultimately leading to a more fulfilled and authentic life.

Envisioning Your Ideal Environment

Thinking about your ideal workplace or community can offer valuable insights into your core values. The way you envision these spaces reveals what's most important to you. Whether collaboration and transparency or competition and ambition, your ideal environment mirrors your deepest beliefs.

Exploring the details of your ideal space helps you understand your values on a deeper level. This process of self-discovery enables you to live more authentically, in alignment with the beliefs that truly drive you.

Reflection Questions

Understanding Your Gift

How do you perceive the idea of being divinely created with unique qualities?

What aspects of your personality or skills feel most aligned with a higher purpose?

How does the concept of a "Divine Blueprint" resonate with you? Do you feel you have discovered yours?

Relating to Life Purpose

What does Jeremiah 29:11 ("For I know the plans I have for you") mean to you personally?

Can you identify moments in your life where you felt guided toward your purpose?

How do the stories of Biblical figures inspire your understanding of living with intentionality?

Recognizing Your Worth

How do you define self-worth, and what role does faith play in shaping it?

In what ways do you currently cultivate a sense of worth in your life?

How does recognizing your worth influence your personal growth and faith journey?

The Role of Identity

What aspects of your identity feel most authentic to you?

How do your aspirations reflect your identity and faith?

---58 -- P a g e -

In what ways does your faith shape how you see yourself and your potential?

Dreaming with Purpose

Are your dreams aligned with your values and faith?

How do your core values guide the decisions you make daily?

What dreams have you set aside, and how can you revisit them with intention and faith?

Living by Your Core Values

What are your top three core values, and how do they influence your life choices?

Can you identify areas in your life where you feel out of alignment with your values?

What practical steps can you take to live more consistently by your core values?

Action Steps

Understanding Your Gift

Reflect on your unique qualities by journaling about times when you felt most fulfilled or impactful.

Read scriptures related to purpose (e.g., Ephesians 2:10, Psalm 139:14) and meditate on their relevance to your life.

Relating to Life Purpose

Write down one or two Biblical figures whose life stories inspire you. Reflect on how their journey relates to your own.

Spend time in prayer or meditation asking for clarity on your purpose and steps to align with it.

Recognizing Your Worth

Make a list of affirmations based on scripture (e.g., "I am fearfully and wonderfully made") and repeat them daily.

Identify three achievements that reflect your strengths and write how they have contributed to your growth.

The Role of Identity

Create a vision board that illustrates your aspirations, core identity, and faith goals.

Write a personal mission statement that reflects your identity, values, and purpose.

Dreaming with Purpose

List your current dreams and assess whether they align with your faith and values. Adjust goals that feel out of sync.

Set SMART goals (Specific, Measurable, Achievable, Relevant, Time-bound) to work toward purposeful aspirations.

Living by Your Core Values

Perform a values audit: Write down your top five values and evaluate whether your daily habits reflect them.

Choose one value to focus on each week and commit to living it out through specific actions.

These reflection questions and action steps aim to deepen your understanding of the chapter while encouraging intentional and faith-based personal growth.

Chapter Two
Building a Foundation of Faith

Preparing for life's disappointments and challenges requires laying a strong foundation of faith before trials arise. However, if such preparation has not been undertaken, now is the ideal moment to build spiritual resilience. This involves creating a firm base to withstand life's inevitable hardships, like constructing a solid foundation for a building that must endure storms and pressures.

To assess and strengthen our foundation, we must first turn to God. By embracing His salvation, repenting sin, and following His guidance, we establish the initial steps of this spiritual base. Maintaining this foundation requires consistent practices like bringing every thought and decision to God, thanking Him for His wisdom, and aligning our lives with His teachings. As Matthew 7:24–25 illustrates, those who build their lives on the "rock" of God's word remain steadfast when rain falls, floods rise, and winds blow. There is no firmer foundation than God Himself, who serves as our ultimate refuge.

Hebrews 11:1 is one of the Bible's most profound and celebrated definitions of faith. It doesn't merely describe faith; it invites us to embody it daily. This verse provides a foundational understanding of living with hope and trust in God, even amidst life's uncertainties.

Rather than being a verse reserved for memorization, Hebrews 11:1 serves as an anchor for our lives. It demonstrates how faith transforms us and continuously points us back to God's promises. Spending time reflecting on its meaning can encourage and deepen our faith. Let's delve into this remarkable verse together.

In Hebrews 10, the focus is on God's unwavering faithfulness. As we move into Hebrews 11, the spotlight shifts to human faithfulness in response. This chapter, often called the "Faith Chapter," presents a vivid definition of faith and provides inspiring examples of what it looks like when lived out. The text doesn't just stop at defining faith; it challenges believers to demonstrate their faith through action and obedience.

Faith, as the author portrays it, is deeply tied to trust. To have faith in God is to place our complete trust in Him. As we examine the meaning of Hebrews 11:1, this essential truth becomes clear.

"Faith is the substance" refers to confidence in what we hope for. Faith is the foundation of the Christian life, built upon the person and work of Jesus Christ. It's through Him that our faith has substance and a firm foundation.

Importantly, this isn't a blind faith. The word "substance" indicates a reasoned and secure confidence rooted in evidence. Christianity offers a faith that is rational and grounded in truth. Believers are called to trust in God because of the solid foundation laid by Christ's life, death, and resurrection.

The Evidence of Things Not Seen

While evidence supports faith, it doesn't give us the full picture. There's confidence in things hoped for yet unseen. The Greek word hypostasis, often translated as "evidence" or "assurance," implies a strong conviction.

Faith enables us to live confidently, even without complete understanding, trusting in God's promises and faithfulness. As Dr. Tom Constable aptly summarizes, "Faith is confidence that things yet future and unseen will happen as God has revealed they will." Faith is not merely a belief but a lived confidence in God's character and promises.

Three Lessons from Hebrews 11:1

1. Place Your Trust in God

Faith, as described in Hebrews 11:1, begins with trust. To trust God means following Him even when circumstances seem unclear or illogical. It involves aligning our actions with His Word and believing His promises will come to fruition. This trust is foundational to our relationship with Him.

2. Look Beyond the Seen

Human nature often tempts us to rely on what we can observe and understand. Yet faith calls us to look beyond our immediate circumstances and focus on God's eternal plan. Hebrews 11:1 encourages us to cling to our hope in God, even when His work remains unseen.

Christians are reminded to hold fast to God's promises and to live by faith rather than sight, as emphasized in 2 Corinthians 5:7: "For we live by faith, not by sight."

3. Cling to Hope in Difficult Times

Trials, grief, and suffering are inevitable, but faith gives us hope even in the darkest seasons. Hebrews 11:1 reassures us that God is faithful and promises remain true. While life may bring hardship, believers are never alone—God is present and will lead them through every struggle.

Jesus promised that He would be with His followers and that all things would be made right one day. This hope anchors us during challenging times, reminding us that our trials are temporary and that we have an eternal future with Him.

Building a foundation of faith is a journey requiring intentional practices that cultivate a deeper relationship with God. Here are practical ways to nurture this foundation:

Study God's Word: Immersing yourself in Scripture provides guidance and wisdom. Proverbs 4:5 encourages us to seek understanding and remember His teachings.

Meditate on Scripture: As Joshua 1:8 highlights, reflecting on God's word daily strengthens your mind and heart.

Develop a Prayer Life: Consistent communication with God builds trust and fosters spiritual intimacy. As 1 Thessalonians 5:17 advises, "pray without ceasing."

Seek Fellowship: Connecting with other believers offers encouragement and accountability, as Hebrews 10:25 reminds us not to forsake gatherings together.

Serve Others: Following Christ's example of selfless service (Mark 10:45) fortifies faith and demonstrates love in action.

Embrace Forgiveness: Practicing forgiveness and reconciliation aligns with God's grace and fosters inner peace (Matthew 6:14).

Trust in God's Plan: Proverbs 3:5–6 calls us to lean on God's understanding and surrender our anxieties to His perfect will.

Seek Wisdom: Proverbs 2:6 affirms that wisdom comes from God, and we should rely on Him for discernment.

Cultivate Gratitude: Even in difficult times, thankfulness deepens trust in God's provision (1 Thessalonians 5:18).

Guard Your Heart: Protecting yourself from negative influences, as advised in Proverbs 4:23, is crucial to maintaining spiritual focus.

Practice Humility: Recognizing God as the source of all blessings nurtures a spirit of humility (Proverbs 11:2).

Share Your Faith: Spreading the Gospel strengthens your convictions and fulfills Christ's commission in Matthew 28:19–20.

Stay Rooted in Christ: As John 15:4 teaches, abiding in Christ keeps you nourished and spiritually vibrant.

Persevere in Trials: Enduring hardships with faith, as James 1:12 describes, refines and strengthens your spiritual foundation.

Love God and Others: Jesus emphasized the importance of loving God wholeheartedly and loving others as ourselves (Matthew 22:37–39).

Building a foundation of faith is not a one-time event but a continual process that integrates prayer, Scripture, and active love. By anchoring your life in these practices, you create a solid spiritual base capable of withstanding any challenge. This allows your faith to flourish and provides strength for yourself and those around you.

How faith provides stability amid uncertainty.

Faith is a cornerstone of stability in a believer's life, offering both spiritual and practical guidance to navigate life's uncertainties. Rooted in an active trust in God's promises and character, faith provides a steadfast anchor even amidst tumultuous circumstances. The Bible consistently portrays faith as essential for cultivating peace, resilience, and a sense of purpose, ultimately enabling believers to maintain stability regardless of external challenges.

Faith as a Firm Foundation

Scripture often highlights faith as the solid groundwork for a stable life. Hebrews 11:1 describes faith as "the assurance of what we hope for and the certainty of what we do not see." This assurance gives believers a sense of security amid life's unpredictable nature. Faith transcends passive belief; it is an active reliance on God, ensuring stability when circumstances seem overwhelming.

Faith and Inner Peace

There is a direct link between faith and peace, an essential element of stability. Isaiah 26:3 promises, "You will keep in perfect peace the steadfast of mind because he trusts in You." External conditions do not influence this peace; they flow from trust in God. It stabilizes the heart and mind, grounding believers in an unwavering calm and confidence.

Faith During Trials

The stabilizing power of faith becomes especially evident in times of hardship. James 1:2-3 urges believers to "consider it pure joy... when you encounter trials of many kinds, because you know that the testing of your faith develops perseverance." Faith equips believers to endure difficulties, transforming challenges into opportunities for growth. Through perseverance, a mature and steadfast character emerges.

Faith and Wisdom

Faith also plays a pivotal role in seeking and applying wisdom, a vital element of stability. James 1:5 encourages, "If any of you lacks wisdom, he should ask God, who gives generously to all without finding fault, and it will be given to him." Seeking wisdom through faith acknowledges God's sovereignty and deepens dependence on His guidance, resulting in decisions that foster stability.

Faith Expressed Through Obedience

Obedience to God's teachings further solidifies the foundation of a believer's life. In Matthew 7:24-25, Jesus likens those who act on His words to a wise man who builds his house on the rock, withstanding life's storms: "The rain fell, the torrents raged, and the winds blew and beat against that house, yet it did not fall, because its foundation was on the rock." Faithful adherence to God's Word creates a life resilient to challenges.

Faith Within Community

Faith also strengthens stability through the support of a faith-based community. Hebrews 10:24-25 exhorts believers to "spur one another on to love and good deeds" and to gather for mutual encouragement. A faith-based community offers support, accountability, and collective stability, reinforcing the individual's trust in God.

Faith and an Eternal Perspective

Finally, faith provides stability by shifting focus to an eternal perspective. As Paul writes in 2 Corinthians 4:17-18, "For our light and momentary affliction is producing an eternal glory far beyond comparison. So we fix our eyes not on what is seen, but on what is unseen." This outlook allows believers to transcend present uncertainties, anchoring their hope in the promise of eternal glory.

The importance of small, consistent acts of trust in God.

The importance of small, consistent acts of trust in God lies in their transformative power to deepen faith, build resilience, and foster a sense of peace. Trusting in God is not just about grand, dramatic gestures or moments of profound revelation—it is often in the small, daily acts of faith that a meaningful relationship with God is cultivated. These acts demonstrate a steady reliance on God's guidance and faithfulness, even in the seemingly mundane aspects of life.

When we choose to trust God in small matters—whether asking for wisdom in a minor decision, thanking Him for daily blessings, or surrendering seemingly insignificant worries—these acts accumulate over time. Like drops of water that eventually fill a jar, these moments create a reservoir of faith that sustains us during life's greater challenges. This consistency nurtures a habit of turning to God, reinforcing our belief that He is present in every detail of our lives.

Small acts of trust also reflect humility and acknowledgment of God's sovereignty. By consistently inviting Him into the everyday, we affirm that we are not self-reliant but are instead guided by a higher power. This humility fosters a sense of peace, knowing we don't have to bear life's burdens alone. It reminds us of God's promises, as stated in Proverbs 3:5-6, to direct our paths when we trust Him wholeheartedly.

Moreover, these small acts can inspire others. When those around us see our quiet confidence and steadfast faith, even in the face of uncertainty, it can encourage them to seek a similar relationship with God. Our consistent trust becomes a testimony to His faithfulness.

Ultimately, small, consistent acts of trust are like planting seeds. Over time, they grow into a robust faith capable of weathering storms. They teach us to rely not on our understanding but on God's perfect wisdom and timing. Through this practice, we learn that faith is not just a destination but a daily journey of aligning our hearts and minds with God's will.

Trusting the Process

Have you ever encountered the phrase "trust the process" and wondered about its significance? This simple yet powerful philosophy encourages resilience, patience, and consistent effort, helping you navigate life's uncertainties while striving for your goals. It's not about passively waiting for success but embracing the journey as a series of small, meaningful steps leading to fulfillment.

What Does It Mean to Trust the Process?

Trusting the process is a mindset of actively working toward your goals while accepting that progress takes time. It requires faith in your efforts and understanding that each step contributes to growth, no matter how small. This approach applies to various life aspects, such as education, career development, personal growth, and relationships. By trusting the process, you learn to focus on the journey rather than being fixated solely on immediate outcomes.

Trusting the process does not mean complacency. Instead, it emphasizes persistent action and a belief that consistent effort leads to success. When results seem distant, this philosophy reminds you that progress often starts with tiny, imperceptible changes—like drops of water that eventually form a mighty ocean.

The Benefits of Trusting the Process

Trusting the process offers numerous advantages that fuel personal growth and success. These include:

Patience and Delayed Gratification

Trusting the process helps you focus on the bigger picture, fosters patience, and teaches the value of delayed gratification. By making sacrifices today, you build a foundation for future rewards, confident that your efforts are not in vain.

Enhanced Focus and Consistency

Maintaining faith in the process keeps you consistent and focused, even when progress seems slow. This consistency is essential for mastering skills and achieving long-term goals.

Reduced Stress and Anxiety

Worrying about immediate results often leads to stress and frustration. Trusting the process shifts your mindset, allowing you to remain calm and focus on productive tasks rather than outcomes beyond your control.

Boosted Confidence

Recognizing and celebrating small achievements reinforces self-belief. Each step forward builds your confidence, motivating you to persist even when faced with challenges.

Self-Discovery

The journey of trusting the process often reveals your strengths, weaknesses, and values. Overcoming obstacles teaches you valuable lessons about yourself and enhances your personal development.

Fostering a Growth Mindset

A growth mindset embraces challenges as opportunities for learning and improvement. Trusting the process nurtures this mindset, helping you view setbacks as stepping stones to success.

Increased Self-Discipline

Trusting the process requires discipline to stay the course. Over time, this discipline becomes a habit that drives you to manage time and energy effectively toward your goals.

Building Resilience

Challenges are inevitable, but trusting the process builds resilience, enabling you to bounce back stronger and continue moving forward despite difficulties.

Learning from Failures

Viewing failures as part of the journey helps you extract lessons from setbacks rather than becoming discouraged. This perspective equips you with the determination to keep striving.

Sustained Motivation

Trusting the process keeps your goals focused, motivating you to persist even when progress is not immediately visible.

How to Embrace and Trust the Process

Adopting this mindset involves specific steps:

Accept the Journey

Success is not an overnight event but a series of cumulative efforts. Each small step you take toward your goal is a success in itself.

Acknowledge Your Starting Point

Recognize where you are and focus on achievable short-term goals. This helps you avoid feeling overwhelmed by the bigger picture.

Believe in Yourself

Confidence in your abilities is crucial. Even when progress seems slow, trust that your efforts will eventually lead to success.

Avoid Comparisons

Comparing your progress to others can be counterproductive. Focus on your unique journey and the milestones you've achieved.

Practice Patience

Growth takes time. Cultivate patience and maintain optimism, knowing every effort contributes to your ultimate goal.

Adapt to Challenges

Embrace change and remain flexible in your approach. Challenges are inevitable in growth, and adapting to them strengthens your resolve.

Learn from Others

Draw inspiration from the experiences of those who have succeeded. Their stories can reinforce your belief in the process and motivate you to keep going.

Doubts and fears arise during the journey.

Doubts and fears are natural companions in pursuing goals and dreams. They often arise uninvited, whispering uncertainties that challenge our resolve. Here's how they might surface in human form:

"Am I doing this right?"

This doubt shows up when progress feels slow and you wonder if your steps are leading anywhere. It questions your methods and makes you second-guess decisions, leaving you hesitant to move forward.

"What if I fail?"

Fear of failure lurks in the shadows, constantly reminding you of the risks involved. It magnifies the consequences of mistakes, making every stumble feel like a disaster waiting to happen.

"Why is this taking so long?"

Impatience speaks up, comparing your timeline to others' and convincing you you're falling behind. It plants the idea that your efforts might not pay off, eroding your perseverance.

"Do I even deserve this?"

Self-doubt becomes a voice of insecurity, asking if you're truly capable or worthy of achieving your dreams. It points out every flaw and every past failure, making it hard to see your strengths.

"What will people think if I don't succeed?"

The fear of judgment stands tall, reminding you of the expectations others might have. It feeds off your vulnerability, making the thought of public failure unbearable.

"Why do others seem to have it so easy?"

Comparison grows louder, drawing your focus to the apparent ease with which others achieve success. It closes your eyes to their struggles and highlights your own perceived inadequacies.

"What if I'm wasting my time?"

Doubt questions the worth of your effort, whispering that you might be chasing something unattainable. It makes you wonder if all your sacrifices and hard work are in vain.

"Am I strong enough to handle this?"

Fear challenges your resilience, casting shadows on your ability to weather setbacks and navigate uncertainty. It makes every obstacle feel insurmountable.

"Will it ever get better?"

When the road gets tough, despair tries to take over, convincing you that the struggle is endless. It makes you question if there's light at the end of the tunnel.

"Should I just give up?"

The loudest fear, the temptation to quit, sneaks in when the journey overwhelms. It promises relief but robs you of the potential for success just around the corner.

These doubts and fears are part of the human experience but don't define the journey. Recognizing them for what they are—temporary and often irrational—can help you move past them. The key is to keep taking small, meaningful steps forward, trusting that persistence and effort will eventually quiet these voices.

Divine Timing

Do you ever wonder if everything in life happens for a reason? Do the opportunities you encounter arrive precisely when you need them? This concept, often called "divine timing," suggests that a higher power—such as the Universe or God—is intricately guiding the course of your life. How can we align ourselves with this celestial guidance? Let's explore.

Divine timing often reveals itself in subtle, almost imperceptible ways—so small that you might overlook them. It's the experience of being "in the right place at the right time" or witnessing life events unfold on a timeline vastly different from what you had planned. This phenomenon reminds us that life's events are not always within our control but may align with a greater design.

For many, divine timing embodies the belief that the Universe operates with wisdom and love, delivering experiences that foster your soul's growth at precisely the right moment. While some embrace the idea that everything happens for a reason, others may view life's events as coincidences. Ultimately, your decision is personal, and either perspective is valid.

For those with a profound spiritual connection, divine timing becomes more than an abstract idea—it's a tangible reminder that the Universe, God, or our spiritual guides are constantly orchestrating circumstances behind the scenes to bring us what we need most. It requires patience and a willingness to surrender to God's timing, trusting that life will unfold as it should.

Patience and Surrender

Trusting in divine timing is often an exercise in patience. It asks us to relinquish the urge to control every outcome and embrace the understanding that not everything happens on our preferred schedule. Surrendering to God's timing involves faith—faith that what is meant for you will not pass you by and that delays may be blessings in disguise.

Real-Life Examples of Divine Timing

Consider these real-life moments of divine timing:

Running into someone who provides exactly the advice or help you need when you're stuck.

Missing a train or plane, only to find that the delay led to an unexpected but pivotal opportunity.

Receiving an unexpected job offer or invitation when you thought doors were closing.

Whether you view these instances as orchestrated by a divine force or simply coincidences, they often remind us to trust the process. By practicing patience and surrendering to a higher power's timeline, we open ourselves to the wisdom and beauty of life's unfolding path.

Life unfolds in seasons, each uniquely interwoven with its challenges and blessings. Ecclesiastes 3:1 beautifully reminds us, "To everything, there is a season and a time to every purpose under the heaven." This verse encourages us to recognize the cyclical nature of life and the divine timing that orchestrates it all. Every moment and every event fits perfectly into the grand tapestry of God's purpose.

Understanding the Seasons of Life

Just as nature transitions through spring, summer, autumn, and winter, our lives ebb and flow through growth, change, rest, and renewal periods. Each season serves a vital role in shaping us and preparing us for what lies ahead.

Spring: A season of beginnings and fresh starts, spring invites us to plant seeds for the future. This might mean starting new projects, forming relationships, or setting fresh goals. It is a time of hope and possibility.

Summer: Marked by growth and productivity, summer is when the seeds of spring take root and flourish. This is a period to nurture our endeavors, embrace joy, and savor the fruits of our labor.

Autumn: A time of change and harvest, autumn allows us to reap what we've sown and reflect on our progress. It's also a season of release as we let go of what no longer serves us, much like trees shedding their leaves in preparation for renewal.

Winter: Winter brings rest and reflection. As the world slows, it offers a sacred pause to rejuvenate, gather strength, and prepare for the next growth cycle.

Reflecting on Your Current Season

Which season of life are you in today? Are you planting seeds, nurturing growth, reaping a harvest, or pausing for renewal? Each season carries its beauty, purpose, and challenges. Embrace where you are with faith, trusting that God's plan for your life is unfolding perfectly.

Prayer for the Seasons

"Lord, thank You for the seasons of life. Help me to discern the season I am in and align myself with Your will. Teach me to trust Your timing, to grow through each phase, and to find peace in Your plan. May I embrace every season with faith and become more like You. Amen."

Action Step: Journaling for Clarity

Take time to journal in prayerful reflection about the season you're experiencing. Consider these questions:

What is God revealing to you in this season?

What lessons are you learning?

What blessings can you count today?

How can you deepen your trust in God during this time?

Use these insights to guide your prayers and shape your actions, allowing God's purpose to shine through each moment.

Closing Thought

Ecclesiastes 3:1 offers a profound reminder that life is ever-changing, but God's presence remains constant. Each season carries a divine purpose; through it, we grow closer to Him. With an open heart, embrace your season, trusting that every moment is part of His plan.

Faith Beyond Fear

James Crockford's collection of sermons stands out for its ability to bring Scripture to life in refreshing and profound ways. With themes ranging from the vast mysteries of cryogenics and UFOs to the familiar beauty of the Red Sea's pink-hued landscape, Crockford's elegant yet approachable reflections offer a renewed perspective on the gospel. Figures like Elijah, John the Baptist, the Blessed Virgin Mary, and Jesus emerge vividly, their stories radiating a light that feels deeply relevant to today's world, as Ayla Lepine, chaplain at King's College, Cambridge, notes.

Martin Seeley, bishop of St. Edmundsbury and Ipswich, commends Crockford's perceptive engagement with resonant life experiences, emphasizing his gift for addressing the heart and mind with humor and grace. This collection fills a notable gap in contemporary sermon literature, offering nourishment for both preachers and seekers of spiritual depth. Angela Tilby, canon emeritus at Christ Church, Oxford, highlights the directness and urgency of these sermons, which remind us that faith calls for transformation. This change is both possible and pressing.

Crockford's ability to focus each sermon on a single, illuminating theme reflects a profound understanding of Christian tradition. As Tilby observes, his learning is never burdensome; instead, it shines a light on the intersection of faith and life's complexities, seeking wholeness rather than conquest. This approach resonates powerfully with the themes explored in Faith Beyond Fear, where the transformative power of faith is examined in the context of overcoming fear and embracing spiritual renewal. Both works invite readers to confront challenges with courage and to discover the potential for change that faith makes possible, illustrating how Scripture and tradition can guide us toward deeper understanding and meaningful action in a fragmented world.

Faith Dismantles Fear: Biblical Lessons and Reassurances

The Scriptures repeatedly affirm that faith in God can dismantle fear, offering comfort, strength, and guidance to those who trust Him. Fear is a universal human experience, often rooted in uncertainty, danger, or the unknown. However, through divine instruction and numerous examples, the Bible encourages believers to confront and overcome fear by anchoring their faith in God's presence and promises.

Biblical Command Against Fear

The Bible consistently calls believers to reject fear, emphasizing reliance on God's omnipresence and power. In Isaiah 41:10, the Lord declares, "Do not fear, for I am with you; do not be dismayed, for I am your God. I will strengthen you, help you; I will uphold you with My right hand of righteousness." This reassurance highlights the divine commitment to support and uplift those who trust in Him, providing a foundation of courage against life's uncertainties.

Similarly, Jesus addresses fear directly in the New Testament. When the disciples are gripped with terror at the sight of Him walking on water, He says in Matthew 14:27, "Take courage! It is I. Do not be afraid." Here, Christ's presence dispels fear, illustrating how faith in His authority brings peace amid chaos.

Faith as a Shield Against Fear

Faith serves as a spiritual shield, guarding believers from fear and doubt. Ephesians 6:16 metaphorically describes this defense: "Take up the shield of faith, with which you can extinguish all the flaming arrows of the evil one." This imagery emphasizes that unwavering trust in God fortifies believers against fear attacks, enabling them to stand firm.

David's encounter with Goliath in 1 Samuel 17 offers a powerful demonstration of faith dismantling fear. Despite the overwhelming odds, David's trust in God's past deliverance gives him the courage to confront the giant. He boldly declares, "The LORD who delivered me from the paw of the lion and the paw of the bear will deliver me from the hand of this Philistine" (1 Samuel 17:37). David's faith in God's power transforms his fear into confidence.

The Role of Prayer in Overcoming Fear

Prayer is a vital practice in dismantling fear through faith. Philippians 4:6-7 urges believers to replace anxiety with prayer: "Do not be anxious about anything, but in every situation, by prayer and petition, with thanksgiving, present your requests to God. And the peace of God, which transcends all understanding, will guard your hearts and minds in Christ Jesus." Through prayer, believers find solace in God's ability to address their fears and grant a supernatural peace that transcends human comprehension.

The Psalms also reflect the power of prayer and trust. In Psalm 56:3-4, the psalmist proclaims, "When I am afraid, I put my trust in You. In God, whose word I praise—in God I trust and am not afraid. What can mere mortals do to me?" This passage reveals the psalmist's reliance on God's character and promises as a source of courage.

Examples of Faith Overcoming Fear

The Bible provides numerous accounts of individuals who dismantled fear through faith. Shadrach, Meshach, and Abednego exemplify unwavering belief in the face of imminent danger. Refusing to bow to Nebuchadnezzar's idol, they declare in Daniel

3:17-18, "If we are thrown into the blazing furnace, the God we serve can deliver us from it... But even if He does not, we want you to know, Your Majesty, that we will not serve your gods." Their faith in God's sovereignty gives them the courage to face death without fear.

Similarly, the apostle Paul demonstrates faith's triumph over fear during a perilous storm at sea. In Acts 27:25, he reassures the crew: "Keep up your courage, men, for I have faith in God that it will happen just as He told me." Paul's unwavering trust in God's promises sustains him and inspires hope and strength in others.

Faith's Transformative Power

The examples and commands in Scripture illustrate that faith is not just a passive belief but an active force that dismantles fear and replaces it with peace, courage, and assurance. By trusting in God's presence, promises, and power, believers can boldly confront life's uncertainties and challenges, knowing that the Almighty upholds them.

Reflection Questions:

How does my faith currently serve as a foundation in my daily life?

Spend time journaling about moments of uncertainty where faith provided stability.

How do I recognize God's presence when outcomes are not visible?

What can I do to strengthen my belief in the unseen?

How do I respond when life doesn't go according to my plans?

What lessons can I learn from moments of uncertainty?

Meditate on scriptures that highlight growth through challenges.

What does trusting in God's timing teach me about patience?

Write about a time when waiting led to a better outcome than rushing.

How can I find purpose and contentment in each season?

Set a goal to embrace the season you're in with faith and intentionality.

Declare affirmations of faith during moments of fear or doubt.

Chapter Three
Vision, Intention, and Action

Intention as the Bridge Between Vision and Action

Intention is the vital link that bridges the clarity of vision with the effectiveness of Action. While vision provides the "why" by outlining a purpose and a sense of direction, and Action constitutes the "how" by translating goals into tangible steps, intention aligns these elements. It ensures that every effort is purposeful and connected to the vision, creating a synergistic relationship where focus, motivation, and energy harmonize to drive progress.

1. Vision Without Intention

The Dreamer's Trap: Vision without intention can lead to idle fantasizing, where grand ideas lack the grounding to manifest into reality. No matter how compelling, a vision remains a distant dream unless coupled with the decisive energy to act. Without intention, it becomes challenging to move from ideation to execution, leaving aspirations unfulfilled.

The Missing Link: Vision defines the destination, but intention fuels the journey. Without the will to act intentionally, vision remains abstract and disconnected from practical, real-world actions.

2. Action Without Intention

Busy Without Purpose: Actions without clear intention can lead to a misallocation of effort. Despite diligent work, the lack of alignment between actions and long-term goals often results in scattered efforts, burnout, and frustration. Purposeful intention prevents this cycle by ensuring actions are tied to meaningful objectives.

Wasted Effort: Reactive, intention less actions may seem productive but often fail to contribute to a broader vision. Without intention as a guiding force, tasks become unstructured and lack meaningful progress.

3. Aligning Vision and Action Through Intention

Clarifying the "Why" Behind the "How": Intention imbues actions with meaning by connecting them to the larger vision. By continuously reflecting on the "why," individuals ensure that each step aligns with their ultimate goals. This Process fosters a deeper sense of purpose, making even small efforts feel significant.

Transforming Ideas into Reality: Vision is the conceptual destination, while intention translates it into actionable steps. This bridge enables individuals to execute their plans with focus and discipline, creating a roadmap from ideation to realization.

Fostering Focus and Motivation: Purpose-driven actions eliminate distractions, enabling a clear focus on what truly matters. Intention provides the clarity to prioritize meaningful tasks, maintaining motivation as each effort contributes to the overarching vision.

4. Sustaining Momentum Through Intention

Navigating Obstacles: Challenges and setbacks are inevitable on the journey toward fulfilling a vision. Intention acts as an anchor, keeping individuals grounded and committed. When obstacles arise, intention ensures adaptability, allowing actions to evolve without losing sight of the ultimate goal.

Maintaining Consistency: Intention promotes discipline and consistency, empowering steady progress even during periods of stagnation. Staying connected to intention prevents feeling overwhelmed by day-to-day demands, enabling sustained momentum.

Creating Flow: When vision and Action are harmonized by intention, individuals often achieve a state of flow where effort feels natural and unforced. This alignment enhances creativity, efficiency, and productivity without unnecessary strain.

5. Practical Steps to Harness Intention

Define Your Vision Clearly: Establish a vivid and precise understanding of the desired future. A clear vision is the foundation for cultivating a strong and effective intention.

Set Daily Intentions: Break down long-term goals into actionable daily intentions. These focused commitments help ground abstract aspirations in immediate, achievable steps, ensuring progress remains tangible.

Align Actions with Core Values: Actions that reflect personal values strengthen the connection between vision and intention.

When actions align with values, they feel more authentic, fostering intrinsic motivation to stay the course.

Use Visualization to Reinforce Intention: Visualization is a powerful tool for mentally rehearsing the future. By imagining desired outcomes, individuals strengthen their focus and align their daily actions with long-term objectives.

Reflect and Reassess: Regular reflection ensures that actions align with vision and intention. This ongoing evaluation process allows individuals to recalibrate as needed, guaranteeing continuous alignment with their goals.

The Synergy of Vision, Intention, and Action

Vision, intention, and Action form a dynamic trio that drives success. Vision defines the destination, intention aligns purpose with effort, and Action brings aspirations to life. Together, they create a feedback loop where intention bridges the gap, ensuring that every effort is meaningful, focused, and impactful. When vision, purpose, and Action align, achieving meaningful goals becomes productive and deeply fulfilling.

Vision Casting

Vision casting is as straightforward as its name implies: it involves crafting a vivid picture of what a better world could look like through the impact of your product or service and then sharing that vision with others to inspire Action. While it might sound simple, many leaders fall into a common trap—they confuse their dreams, vision, and mission. This muddling creates uncertainty, leaving teams unclear about where they are headed, why the journey matters, and how to get there. To avoid this, it's essential to distinguish between dreams, vision, and mission and understand how they guide your business.

Dreams

Dreams are the initial sparks of possibility—the big "what ifs" that hit you in moments of inspiration, like during a shower or after your morning coffee. These ideas are important because they signify belief in your potential and your business. However, dreams alone won't move you forward. Without a clear vision to guide them, dreams remain static and unfulfilled. Just as imagining a roasted duck doesn't make one appear, merely dreaming about success won't bring your ideas to life. Vision is the missing link to transform dreams into reality.

Vision

Vision is the bridge between your dreams and reality. It is the ability to see what you hope to achieve and develop actionable plans to make it happen. Unlike dreams, vision requires focus and structure. It is deeply rooted in the purpose of your business and serves as a roadmap to success. A strong vision motivates and creates a sense of direction and alignment, ensuring that your team knows where they are headed and how their efforts contribute to the bigger picture.

Mission

Your mission is your organization's core, the heartbeat that drives everything you do. It defines who you are, what you stand for, and why you exist. The mission acts as a compass, ensuring that every vision you cast and decision you make aligns with your core purpose. For example, LinkedIn's mission is to connect professionals globally to enhance productivity and success, while its vision expands this goal to create economic opportunities for every workforce member. Together, their mission and vision provide clarity, focus, and direction.

Practical Tips for Vision Casting

Write It Down

Vision casting begins with documentation. Whether it's a detailed vision statement or a vision board filled with images and words, writing it down makes your goals tangible and visible. For instance, a client achieving a speaking opportunity they placed on their vision board is a powerful reminder of how writing and visualizing your goals can lead to fulfillment.

Write in Past Tense, Not Future

Frame your vision as though it has already happened to instill confidence and clarity. For example, instead of saying, "I will increase sales," write, "By June 15th, I increased sales by 25%." This approach creates a sense of achievement and momentum toward your goals.

Use Vivid and Emotional Descriptions

Paint your vision with descriptive language and emotions to bring it to life. Imagine a vibrant and collaborative workspace filled with creativity and joy. In 2014, envisioning such a space led to creating a dog-friendly, award-winning office with a culture of collaboration and positivity—a direct result of thoughtful vision casting.

Share Your Vision

Sharing your vision with others is vital. Conversations about your goals can spark unexpected opportunities. For example, a casual lunch discussion about transitioning from a virtual operation to a physical office space led to a client generously offering free office space. This act of generosity arose simply because the vision was shared.

Why Vision Casting Works

Although there may not be a scientific explanation, the power of vision casting is evident in its results. History and experience show its importance. As Will Rogers famously said, "Even if you're on the right track, you'll get run over if you just stand there." Vision casting propels you forward, ensuring you don't remain stagnant but actively pursue personal and professional growth.

Vision casting transforms vague aspirations into a clear, actionable roadmap that motivates and aligns everyone involved. By distinguishing dreams, vision, and mission and embracing the art of vision casting, you can drive your business toward success while inspiring others to join you on the journey.

The Role of Vision in Spiritual and Personal Growth

Vision and hope are foundational to spiritual growth and maturity, igniting believers' passion and determination to align their lives with God's purposes. Vision provides clarity and focus, acting as a compass that guides Christians toward living according to God's will. It serves as a vital link in the profound journey of spirituality, transcending simple definitions to encompass the essence of conscious existence—a connection to the broader universe that fosters an enriched understanding of one's place.

Individual Paths to Spiritual Awareness

Spiritual awareness is a deeply personal experience that varies significantly from one individual to another. Unlike a universal roadmap, it is shaped by unique beliefs, values, and life experiences. This diversity underscores that there is no singularly "correct" way to attain spiritual enlightenment.

Distinguishing Religion from Spirituality

A common misconception intertwines spirituality with religion, yet the two concepts are distinct. Religion typically refers to organized systems of doctrines, rituals, and practices to foster collective worship. In contrast, spirituality is an inward exploration of meaning, purpose, and connection to a higher power, promoting personal introspection and a deeper understanding of life. Vision plays a key role here, encouraging individuals to focus on their spiritual growth and align their practices with their core values.

Personal Growth and Spiritual Development

Personal growth represents a holistic journey of self-improvement encompassing emotional, physical, and spiritual dimensions. It involves learning new skills, cultivating emotional intelligence, and embracing self-awareness. Spirituality, focusing on inner connection and wisdom, becomes a vital catalyst for this growth. Vision ties these elements together, providing the clarity needed to define personal goals and persevere through challenges.

Emotional Detachment and Tranquility

Emotional detachment is crucial for maintaining poise and tranquility amid life's uncertainties. Spirituality is pivotal in fostering this equilibrium by promoting practices such as mindfulness and gratitude. These practices, guided by vision, nurture resilience and acceptance, essential for personal growth.

The Union of Spirituality and Vision in Growth

Spirituality enriches personal development by illuminating life's purpose and strengthening one's values, principles, and aspirations. Vision enhances this Process by offering a clear perspective on goals and motivating individuals to pursue them with intent and resilience. As spiritual practices deepen, self-awareness expands, laying the foundation for transformative growth.

Health Benefits of Spiritual Growth

The intersection of spirituality, vision, and self-awareness initiates profound changes that positively impact emotional, mental, and physical well-being. Spiritual practices such as gratitude, meditation, and mindfulness promote inner peace and enhance emotional stability, interpersonal relationships, and coping mechanisms. Vision amplifies these benefits by encouraging consistency and intentionality in these practices, leading to meaningful improvements in overall health and well-being.

Overcoming Spiritual Depression

In today's demanding world, faith can waver, often leading to spiritual depression. However, a clear vision and renewed spiritual practices can restore hope and purpose, reigniting the journey toward growth and fulfillment.

The Synergy of Vision and Spiritual Practices

Ultimately, the power of vision lies in its ability to harmonize spirituality and personal growth. By fostering a strong sense of purpose, vision inspires believers to navigate life's challenges with grace and determination. It empowers individuals to embrace their spiritual journeys, deepening self-awareness, enhancing resilience, and unlocking their full potential. In doing so, vision becomes a transformative force, uniting spirituality and personal growth into a cohesive and enriching experience.

Strategies For Crafting A God-Centered Vision

Crafting a vision for your life and business is more than setting goals—it's about aligning your personal and professional aspirations with God's divine purpose. A well-defined, God-centered vision becomes a guiding light, offering clarity, direction, and motivation as you pursue the dreams God has planted in your heart. Here, we'll explore actionable strategies for creating a powerful, God-centered vision that inspires and guides every step of your journey.

1. Seeking Divine Guidance for Your Vision

A God-centered vision begins with understanding His plan for your life. Start by reflecting on your core values—those guiding principles that shape your decisions and interactions. Ask God to reveal the values that align with His truth, allowing them to anchor your decisions.

Next, consider your unique purpose: how God has called you to impact the world. Reflect on how your talents, passions, and experiences fit His plan. Questions like, "What does God want me to contribute? How can I serve others while honoring Him?" help clarify your purpose. Rooting your vision in God's calling creates a foundation strong enough to endure challenges and setbacks.

2. Imagining a God-Centered Future

Spend time visualizing the life God desires for you. Picture every facet—your relationships, work, health, and spiritual growth—with God at the center. As you brainstorm, write down everything that resonates, trusting that God's plans surpass what you can imagine (Ephesians 3:20).

Prioritize elements that reflect your values and purpose. This exercise narrows your focus, making it easier to set meaningful goals that align with God's intentions.

3. Creating Your Personal Vision Statement

Translate your reflections into a life vision statement that captures your aspirations and God's purpose. This statement should be clear, concise, and Christ-centered, serving as a daily reminder of the journey God has called you to undertake. A strong vision statement inspires consistency and aligns your decisions with His will.

4. Crafting a God-Centered Vision for Your Business

Your business, like your life, should reflect God's values. Begin by defining your business purpose beyond profit. Consider how your business can serve others, embody integrity, and demonstrate God's love and excellence in the marketplace.

Visualize your ideal business, imagining its culture, operations, customer interactions, and impact. Pray for guidance as you dream big, trusting that God's plans for your work are purposeful and transformative.

5. Establishing a Business Culture Rooted in Faith

Culture shapes the heartbeat of your business. To create a God-centered culture, prioritize integrity, humility, service, and compassion. As a leader, let these principles guide your decisions and interactions. A faith-driven culture not only sets your business apart but also ensures that it honors God in every aspect.

6. Writing a Business Vision Statement

Your business vision statement should articulate what your company aspires to become, rooted in God's purpose. This statement guides decision-making, inspires your team, and aligns everyone with a shared mission. Additionally, write a detailed summary of your ideal business to create a vivid narrative that keeps you and your team motivated as you pursue God-given goals.

7. Harmonizing Personal and Professional Visions

A fulfilling life requires harmony between your personal and business aspirations. Review your life and business vision statements to identify conflicts or areas of misalignment. For instance, if your personal vision emphasizes family time while your business demands extensive travel, explore ways to reduce travel or make trips more meaningful. Finding synergy between the two visions ensures balance and alignment with God's purpose.

8. Living Your Vision Daily

A God-centered vision is not just an abstract idea—it's a way of life. Incorporate your vision into daily actions, ensuring they align with your values and long-term goals. Establish habits such as prayer, strategic planning, and intentional relationship-building that reflect your vision. By living out your vision, you stay grounded in God's calling and maintain focus on His plan.

9. Revisiting and Refining Your Vision

As you grow in faith and experience, your vision may evolve. Regularly revisit it to ensure it remains aligned with God's will. Update it as needed, keeping it relevant to your season of life and business. Remember, your vision is a living document—a dynamic guide that reflects your journey with God.

Strategies for Crafting a God-Centered Vision

Pray for Guidance: Seek God's wisdom at every stage of crafting your vision, asking Him to reveal His purpose for your life and work.

Reflect on Scripture: Use biblical principles as a foundation for your vision. Verses such as Proverbs 16:3, "Commit to the Lord whatever you do, and He will establish your plans," can inspire trust and direction.

Incorporate Feedback: Consult mentors, spiritual advisors, or trusted peers for insight and affirmation, ensuring your vision aligns with God's Word.

Write and Review: Document your vision clearly and revisit it regularly, allowing it to inspire and guide your decisions.

You create a roadmap that leads to fulfillment, balance, and eternal impact by grounding your life and business vision in God's purpose. Let this Process be a testament to God's guidance in every aspect of your journey.

Spiritual Discernment

When you hear the term "spiritual discernment," what comes to mind? Perhaps you associate it with making pivotal life choices, such as selecting a spouse or choosing a career path. You might envision it as a divine ability to distinguish between good and evil forces in the world. Alternatively, you could see it as the wisdom to comprehend and apply the teachings of Scripture.

Spiritual discernment encompasses all these elements and more, depending on the circumstances. At its core, spiritual discernment is evaluating moral and spiritual matters with insight and attentiveness. It requires deliberate effort and an ongoing commitment to understanding the truth. This Process involves assessing the moral and spiritual state of individuals, groups, or movements guided by biblical principles.

In Matthew 7:1-2, Jesus cautions us to exercise discernment while avoiding judgmental attitudes: "For in the same way you judge others, you will be judged, and with the measure you use, it will be measured to you." The essence of discernment is to navigate decisions and spiritual realities without falling into the trap of judgmentalism.

During His ministry, Jesus demonstrated profound discernment, delving deeply into the essence of matters and responding with wisdom and compassion. Christian believers are called to emulate this discernment, which stems from an intimate connection with God and a commitment to His word. It involves seeing the world through God's perspective and acting accordingly.

Contrary to some misconceptions, spiritual discernment is not merely a mystical awareness of good and evil. It is rooted in wisdom, enabling us to differentiate between right and wrong and align our actions with God's will. As we grow in understanding and obedience to Scripture, we develop the ability to discern moral and spiritual truths effectively.

The Role of Logic and Emotion in Discernment

Decision-making often involves balancing logic (logos) and emotion (ethos). Logical thinkers rely on rationality and objectivity, while emotional thinkers are empathetic and passionate. Both approaches have strengths and weaknesses, but true discernment integrates these perspectives. By harmonizing logic and empathy, we can make sound decisions that honor reason and compassion.

Biblical Examples of Discernment

The Bible offers numerous examples of discernment in Action. Jesus used discernment to heal, teach, and confront spiritual realities. Consider the following verses that highlight the **importance of discernment:**

"Beloved, do not believe every spirit but test the spirits to see whether they are from God, for many false prophets have gone out into the world" (1 John 4:1).

"Do not be conformed to this world, but be transformed by the renewal of your mind, that by testing you may discern what the will of God is, what is good and acceptable and perfect" (Romans 12:2).

"The fear of the Lord is the beginning of knowledge, but fools despise wisdom and instruction" (Proverbs 1:7).

These passages underscore the need for spiritual discernment as a vital aspect of Christian living.

Cultivating Spiritual Discernment

Developing spiritual discernment requires practice and intentionality. Here are some practical steps:

Pray for Guidance

Regular prayer is essential for cultivating discernment. Ask God for wisdom and clarity in decision-making, trusting that He will provide direction. Faith in God's guidance strengthens our ability to make wise choices.

Study Scripture

Immersing yourself in God's word provides a foundation for discernment. By reflecting on biblical teachings and examples, you gain insight into God's will and learn to distinguish right from wrong.

Practice Listening

Spiritual discernment involves attentiveness to God's voice, whether through Scripture, prayer, or life experiences. Meditative prayer and seeking counsel from spiritually mature individuals can enhance your ability to hear and respond to God's guidance.

Avoid Judgmental Attitudes

Discernment is not about passing judgment on others but seeking truth and making righteous decisions. As Jesus reminds us in Matthew 7:1-2, the standard we use to judge others will be applied to us.

Spiritual discernment equips us to navigate life's complexities with wisdom and grace. By integrating prayer, Scripture, and thoughtful decision-making, we align ourselves with God's will and grow in our ability to see the world through His eyes. This practice allows us to act justly, love mercy, and walk humbly with God, fulfilling the call to live in spiritual harmony.

Clarifying Your Goals

Clarity and Vision: Key Ingredients for Achieving Your Goals

In many industries, particularly those focusing on self-improvement or home improvement, clarity and vision are often used interchangeably. However, they serve distinct yet interconnected purposes when pursuing significant goals—such as simplifying your life, living intentionally, or embarking on a new career. Understanding the nuances between clarity and vision can profoundly impact how effectively you achieve your objectives.

The Role of Vision

Vision is the driving force that shapes your decision-making process and narrows your focus. It provides a sense of direction and defines what success looks and feels like. Whether it involves imagining how a decluttered home feels or envisioning the satisfaction of reaching a career milestone, your vision serves as a motivational beacon. For instance, envisioning the purpose of a space or task gives you a clearer picture of your destination, thus helping reduce overwhelm.

While vision contributes to clarity, it is not synonymous with it. Vision is an essential component of clarity, but achieving true clarity requires more—it involves understanding your values, strengths, and purpose.

Values: The Foundation of Clarity

Values are at the heart of clarity, acting as guiding principles that inform your priorities. Knowing what you value enhances your ability to make decisions aligned with your core beliefs. This alignment leads to a greater sense of purpose, fulfillment, and satisfaction. Conversely, a lack of clarity about your values can result in feeling lost or unfulfilled, making decision-making more challenging. By identifying and embracing your values, you can navigate life's decisions more effectively, aligning your actions with what truly matters to you.

Strengths: Leveraging Your Natural Talents

Recognizing and embracing your strengths is another crucial element of clarity. Your strengths encompass your natural abilities, talents, and the activities you excel at and enjoy. Understanding these allows you to make informed decisions about your career and personal life, ensuring your efforts align with tasks that energize and fulfill you. For instance, focusing on roles or projects that capitalize on your strengths increases the likelihood of success and satisfaction. When you harness your strengths, you position yourself to achieve the ultimate goal of being authentically and confidently "you."

Clarity as the Cornerstone of Goal Setting

Clarity is indispensable when setting and achieving goals. Through my experience coaching clients, I've seen how a lack of clarity often undermines goal achievement. Whether breaking a habit, improving creativity, advancing professionally, or enhancing relationships, a clear understanding of what you want to achieve and why is paramount.

For example, a recent client sought support as an accountability coach to develop a daily running habit. When I asked her about her "why," she admitted her motivation stemmed from seeing a friend post about running on Instagram; while this was a starting point, it lacked the depth needed to inspire consistent Action. Without a clear purpose, she experienced decision fatigue—questioning whether to run each morning and eventually giving in to inertia.

Purpose + Vision: A Powerful Combination

As illustrated in the example above, having a tangible outcome and a clear purpose can eliminate many obstacles to goal achievement. Stephen Covey's principle of "beginning with the end in mind" emphasizes the value of envisioning your desired result. A clear vision helps you focus on the outcome, motivating you to persevere through challenges.

Imagine the client had articulated a vision of running five kilometers and visualized the pride, physical strength, and celebration accompanying that milestone. This detailed vision could have ignited her motivation and anchored her daily decisions, making overcoming the temptation to skip her run easier.

Clarity Without Vision

If crafting a detailed vision feels overwhelming due to life's complexities, you can still pursue greater clarity without it. Here are five strategies to enhance clarity:

Take a mental break: Engage in activities like meditation, spending time in nature, or walking to clear your mind.

Ask reflective questions: Consider questions like "What matters most to me right now?" or "What does success look like in this area?"

Seek input from others: Trusted friends, family, or a professional coach can offer valuable perspectives and help you explore your thoughts.

Write it out: Journaling can provide clarity by helping you articulate and organize your thoughts.

Visualize your future self: Imagine achieving your goal and reflect on what steps brought you there.

Clarity and Goal Achievement

Clarity is essential for success in all areas of life, from personal development to professional growth. A clear understanding of your values, strengths, and purpose allows you to navigate challenges with focus and intention. While vision amplifies clarity, both are vital for staying motivated and confident.

Remember that clarity is not a one-time achievement as you work toward your goals. It is an evolving process requiring continuous reflection and adjustment. By aligning your actions with your values and maintaining a clear sense of purpose, you can live a fulfilling, purposeful life.

By relating this approach to clarifying your goals, you can create a structured path that helps eliminate ambiguity, sustain motivation, and achieve meaningful success.

Proverbs 16:3 states, "Commit to the Lord whatever you do, and he will establish your plans" (NIV). This verse highlights the importance of aligning your goals and efforts with a higher purpose, trusting that when you submit your plans to God, He will guide and bless your endeavors.

In the context of goal-setting, this proverb emphasizes three key principles:

1. Alignment with Purpose

When setting goals, it's essential to align them with your values, beliefs, and purpose. By committing your plans to God, you seek divine guidance, ensuring your goals align with a meaningful and righteous path. This step fosters clarity and helps you prioritize what truly matters.

2. Trust in the Process

Committing your goals to God requires trust—both in His wisdom and in the timing of the outcomes. Goal-setting often involves challenges and uncertainty, but by trusting that God will "establish your plans," you find peace and confidence, knowing you are not navigating the journey alone.

3. Active Commitment

The verse uses the word "commit," which implies Action and dedication. While trust in God is vital, this does not negate personal responsibility. It encourages diligent effort and discipline, knowing that your work, guided by faith, will yield fruit.

For example, if your goal is to advance your career or improve your health, Proverbs 16:3 reminds you to involve God in the Process. This could mean seeking wisdom through prayer, acting ethically, and trusting that the outcomes will align with His will, even if they look different than expected.

By incorporating Proverbs 16:3 into your goal-setting Process, you embrace a balanced approach—dedicating your plans to God while taking actionable steps, confident that He will guide you toward a purposeful and fulfilling outcome.

Intentional Living

Intentional living is a deliberate approach to life, characterized by mindfulness, self-awareness, and purposeful Action. It requires stepping away from the automatic routines of life and immersing oneself fully in the present moment. This mindset fosters a deeper connection to life's intricacies, allowing individuals to embrace both its beauty and challenges.

The Holistic Nature of Intentional Living

Living intentionally involves nurturing the harmony between the mind, body, emotions, and spirit. By prioritizing this balance, individuals can cultivate healthier lifestyles and more profound happiness. Intentional living emphasizes emotional wellness, resilience, and mindfulness—skills that equip people to navigate life's complexities with strength and adaptability.

One key component is focusing on what is within one's control. By consciously managing reactions and choices, people can overcome feelings of helplessness, gaining clarity and a sense of empowerment. This approach aligns with the concept of defining one's personal "North Star"—a guiding set of values that directs decisions and actions.

The Mental Health Connection

Intentional living has profound benefits for mental health. Research supports that aligning daily actions with personal values can reduce stress and enhance well-being. A 2021 study revealed that participants who engaged in values-based actions experienced lower daily distress and greater overall happiness. Similarly, a 2019 study among college students found that values-based living improved their ability to cope with stressful events. Intentional practices are even embedded in therapeutic approaches for conditions like anxiety and depression, further underscoring their significance.

Therapists and authors like Lisa Olivera highlight the agency and empowerment derived from intentional living. By fostering presence, self-acceptance, and connection to one's inner power, this lifestyle leads to meaning, fulfillment, and a sense of purpose.

Why Intentional Living Matters

In a world grappling with rising mental health concerns, intentional living offers a beacon of hope. Statistics show alarming rates of anxiety and depression across age groups. For instance, 63% of college students report overwhelming anxiety, and one in three adolescents is likely to experience an anxiety disorder. This mental health crisis underscores the urgency for individuals to prioritize emotional well-being and take personal responsibility for their mental health.

By adopting intentional practices, individuals not only improve their own lives but also positively influence their families, communities, and society. Simple strategies such as mindfulness, emotional regulation, and setting intentions can pave the way for transformative changes.

Practical Strategies for Intentional Living

1. Foundation Building:

Prioritize Wellness: Make mental and emotional health as important as daily obligations like work or errands.

Self-Reflection: Recognize and celebrate personal strengths, passions, and values.

Set Intentions: Define how you want to show up in life, aligning actions with core beliefs.

2. Everyday Strategies:

Guard Your Time: Focus on activities that uplift you while saying no to distractions.

Practice Mindfulness: Slow down to enjoy life's small moments, which re-center and ground you.

Mind Your Language: Embrace positive and empowering phrases to shift your mindset.

Clean Up Your Environment: Declutter social media and other distractions to support mental clarity.

Learn from Others: Seek inspiration and actionable insights from those living the life you aspire to.

Prioritize Rest: Emphasize sleep and self-care for sustainable energy and mental clarity.

Aligned Action: Take steps consistent with your values and long-term goals.

Relating Intentional Living to Broader Wellness

Intentional living reflects the philosophy of creating a purposeful, values-driven life. By consciously designing daily habits and making choices that align with long-term aspirations, individuals cultivate emotional strength, reduce stress, and build resilience. The ripple effect of such practices extends beyond personal well-being, enriching relationships, and contributing to a healthier, more compassionate world.

Embracing the Journey

Living intentionally is an ongoing journey rather than a fixed destination. It begins with small steps, like setting intentions, practicing mindfulness, and reevaluating priorities. These practices transform daily life into a reflection of one's deepest values and aspirations. As you commit to this path, the rewards of enhanced fulfillment, emotional resilience, and a profound sense of purpose will manifest, illuminating the way forward.

For a guided start, consider tools like an intention-setting workbook to clarify goals and establish actionable steps toward living intentionally.

How Intentional Actions Align With Faith

Living Intentionally: A Biblical Perspective

Living intentionally means embracing a life of purpose and deliberate Action. In today's fast-paced and distraction-filled world, intentionality enables us to align our decisions and behaviors with our values and priorities. The Bible encourages believers to live intentionally, rooted in godly principles and mindful choices that honor God while serving others. This guide explores biblical perspectives on intentional living, highlighting key verses, examples, benefits, challenges, and practical tips for cultivating a purposeful life centered on faith.

Defining Intentionality from a Biblical Perspective

The Meaning of Intentionality

Biblical intentionality involves consciously aligning choices, actions, and attitudes with God's principles. Rather than passively navigating life, intentional living demands thoughtful direction and purpose. As Jesus reminds us in John 15:16, "You did not choose me, but I chose you and appointed you so that you might go and bear fruit—fruit that will last." This verse underscores the importance of deliberately ordering our lives to fulfill God's purposes.

Key Verses on Intentional Living

The Bible offers numerous insights into intentional living:

Proverbs 4:26-27: "Give careful thought to the paths for your feet and be steadfast in all your ways. Do not turn to the right or the left; keep your foot from evil." This verse urges careful consideration of our choices to stay aligned with God's will.

Psalm 90:12: "Teach us to number our days, that we may gain a heart of wisdom." Acknowledging the brevity of life encourages the intentional use of time to honor God.

1 Corinthians 14:40: "But everything should be done in a fitting and orderly way." This emphasizes organizing life with purpose and discipline.

How Intentionality Aligns with Biblical Values

Intentional living reflects several core biblical values:

Stewardship: Using gifts, resources, and time wisely for God's glory (1 Peter 4:10).

Wisdom: Evaluating priorities and decisions through the lens of Scripture.

Excellence: Doing everything wholeheartedly for God (Colossians 3:23).

Self-Control: Disciplining desires and actions to align with God's will (Galatians 5:22-23).

Intentionality centers on pursuing God's purposes wholeheartedly and trusting His plans for our lives (Jeremiah 29:11).

Examples of Intentional Living in the Bible

Jesus' Purposeful Ministry

Jesus modeled intentionality throughout His ministry. He selected disciples thoughtfully (Luke 6:12-16), prioritized spreading the Gospel despite challenges (Mark 1:35-39), and resolutely set His face toward Jerusalem to fulfill His mission (Luke 13:31-33). His deliberate actions culminated in His ultimate sacrifice, declaring, "It is finished" (John 19:30).

Paul's Missionary Journeys

The Apostle Paul exemplified intentionality by strategically planting churches in key cities during his missionary journeys. Despite hardships, he stayed focused on spreading the Gospel, as seen in his extended ministry in Corinth (Acts 18:11). His persistence helped establish Christianity's global reach (2 Corinthians 11:23-28).

Ruth's Commitment to Naomi

Ruth's steadfast loyalty to Naomi illustrates intentional care. Despite the personal loss, Ruth chose to support Naomi, gleaning in Boaz's fields to provide for them both. Her purposeful actions brought about God's plan for her role in Jesus' lineage (Ruth 1:16-18).

Benefits of Leading an Intentional Life

Deepening Your Relationship with God

Setting time aside for prayer, Bible study, and worship fosters intimacy with God. Intentional practices enable us to discern His will, experience His faithfulness, and grow in Christlikeness (2 Corinthians 3:18).

Serving Others Effectively

An intentional life equips us to serve others with compassion and foresight. Planning ahead allows us to steward time and resources wisely, meeting significant needs and reflecting God's love (Galatians 6:9).

Setting a Godly Example

A deliberate, God-centered lifestyle inspires others to seek a deeper relationship with Him. Our priorities and reliance on God's guidance model a life devoted to His glory.

Challenges of Intentional Living

Overcoming Distractions

The modern world bombards us with distractions, from constant notifications to fleeting passions. Intentionality requires discipline to focus on meaningful activities that align with God's purposes (Ephesians 5:15-16).

Combating Fleeting Passions

Temporary cravings often lead us away from lasting fulfillment. Recognizing and resisting these impulses helps us prioritize enduring goals over fleeting desires.

Making Time for Reflection

Intentional living demands regular self-examination. Practices such as journaling, prayer, and solitude provide clarity, enabling us to realign with God's priorities amidst life's busyness.

Tips for Cultivating Intentionality

Start with Prayer and Scripture

Begin each day by seeking God's guidance through prayer and Scripture. Apps like Bible.com provide resources for consistent Bible reading to shape your focus (Ephesians 5:15-17).

Define Your Values and Priorities

Identify what matters most to you through reflection and create personal mission statements. Revisiting these periodically helps ensure alignment with your goals.

Build Habits That Reflect Faith

Develop routines that honor God, such as setting aside time for worship, serving others, and pursuing spiritual growth. Tools like habit-tracking apps can support consistency.

Align Actions with Faith

View every choice as an opportunity to glorify God. Whether managing time, relationships, or resources, let biblical principles guide your decisions.

Intentional living rooted in faith transforms our character, strengthens our relationship with God, and equips us to serve others meaningfully. By seeking His wisdom and aligning with His purposes, we can lead lives that honor Him in every season.

Action Plans for Purpose

An action plan is a comprehensive roadmap that outlines the specific steps required to achieve a defined goal or objective. It functions much like a GPS, providing clear directions from your current position to your desired destination. Developing an action plan involves breaking a larger goal into smaller, actionable tasks, making the Process less overwhelming and more manageable. The first step is to clearly define your goal, ensuring it is specific, measurable, achievable, relevant, and time-bound (SMART). For instance, instead of vaguely aiming to "improve sales," you could set a target to "increase sales by 20% within six months," giving you a focused objective and a way to measure progress.

Once the goal is defined, identify the tasks needed to achieve it. These tasks can be subdivided into smaller, actionable items for clarity. For example, to boost sales, you might focus on improving your online presence by updating your website and optimizing it for search engines, conducting targeted email campaigns, or offering promotions to attract new customers. Establishing a timeline with clear deadlines for each task ensures progress can be monitored effectively. If working as part of a team, assign tasks based on individual strengths and responsibilities, fostering accountability and ensuring clarity about who is responsible for what.

Regular monitoring and evaluation of the plan are essential. Review completed tasks and reflect on challenges or delays, making adjustments where necessary to improve effectiveness. An action plan is not static; it evolves with the project, adapting to unforeseen circumstances and maintaining alignment with the overarching goal.

let check lessons from nehemiah's rebuilding of the wall (nehemiah 2).

After months of fervent prayer, Nehemiah approached King Artaxerxes Longimanus I to seek permission to assist the Jews. Through Nehemiah's faith and leadership, God provides seven lessons on Spirit-led leadership: (1) courage of faith, (2) constant prayer, (3) sacrificial service, (4) vigilance, (5) strategic planning, (6) encouragement, and (7) perseverance.

1. Courage of Faith: Acting with Faith-Driven Boldness

Nehemiah demonstrated immense courage when he approached the Persian king without prior authorization—a bold act that could have cost him his life. Despite his fear, Nehemiah pleaded for his people:

"In the month of Nisan, in the twentieth year of King Artaxerxes, when wine was brought for him, I took the wine and gave it to the king. I had not been sad in his presence before, so the king asked me, 'Why does your face look so sad when you are not ill? This can be nothing but sadness of heart.' I was very much afraid." (Neh. 2:1-2).

As the king's cupbearer, Nehemiah held a privileged yet precarious role. His actions paralleled Queen Esther's, who also risked her life to intercede for the Jews (Esth. 4:11-14). Nehemiah's faith exemplifies the truth of Psalm 118:6: "The Lord is with me; I will not be afraid. What can mere mortals do to me?" Spirit-led leaders can take bold steps when they trust God's presence and sovereignty (Rom. 8:31; Is. 41:10).

2. Constant Prayer: Dependence on God through Prayer

Nehemiah was a man of continual prayer. After four months of intercession for the Jews, he prayed once more before presenting his request to the king:

"The king said to me, 'What is it you want?' Then I prayed to the God of heaven, and I answered the king…" (Neh. 2:4-5).

This final, spontaneous prayer reveals Nehemiah's reliance on God for wisdom and favor. Prayer empowered Nehemiah to act boldly yet humbly, trusting God's guidance in every step. His intercessory prayers echo those of other biblical leaders like Abraham (Gen. 18:23), Moses (Ex. 32:11-14), and the apostles (1 Thess. 3:10). James 5:16 reminds us that "The prayer of a righteous person is powerful and effective." Spirit-led leaders should cultivate a life of prayer, bringing every decision before God.

3. Sacrificial Service: A Willingness to Serve at Personal Cost

Nehemiah willingly left his privileged position in the royal court to serve the Jews. He asked the king:

"If it pleases the king… send me to the city in Judah where my ancestors are buried so that I can rebuild it." (Neh. 2:5).

This request reflected Nehemiah's readiness to sacrifice comfort, safety, and status for God's purpose. His willingness mirrors the ultimate example of Jesus, who came not to be served but to serve (Mark 10:45). Spirit-led leaders must be willing to set aside personal gain to fulfill God's call.

4. Vigilance: Preparedness for Opposition

Upon arriving in Jerusalem, Nehemiah encountered immediate opposition from enemies who sought to derail his mission. However, he prepared for resistance by relying on God's protection and implementing practical strategies. Spirit-led leaders recognize the inevitability of challenges and respond with vigilance, trusting God while preparing wisely for adversity (Eph. 6:10-18).

5. Strategic Planning: Acting with Prudence and Vision

Before initiating the rebuilding process, Nehemiah scouted the city and devised a plan:

"I went to Jerusalem, and after staying there three days, I set out during the night with a few others. I had not told anyone what my God had put in my heart to do for Jerusalem." (Neh. 2:11-12).

Through careful planning, Nehemiah exemplified the principle that Spirit-led leadership requires discernment, vision, and preparation. Proverbs 16:9 affirms that "The heart of man plans his way, but the Lord establishes his steps."

6. Encouragement: Inspiring Others to Faith and Action

Nehemiah inspired the people to rebuild the city walls by sharing his testimony of God's faithfulness:

"I also told them about the gracious hand of my God on me and what the king had said to me. They replied, 'Let us start rebuilding.'" (Neh. 2:18).

Through encouragement, Spirit-led leaders motivate others to trust God and take Action. Sharing personal experiences of God's provision and guidance can build faith within a community.

7. Perseverance: Remaining Faithful Amid Opposition

Despite relentless mockery and threats from opponents, Nehemiah persevered in his mission:

"They all plotted together to come and fight against Jerusalem and stir up trouble against it. But we prayed to our God and posted a guard day and night to meet this threat." (Neh. 4:8-9).

Nehemiah's determination underscores the importance of steadfast faith. Spirit-led leaders trust God to provide strength and victory even in the face of adversity (2 Tim. 1:7; Gal. 6:9).

God's plans, especially during times of difficulty and opposition? Following Nehemiah's example, spirit-led leadership involves consistently motivating and uplifting others through testimony, prayer, and reliance on God's guidance. By focusing on a shared mission and emphasizing God's role in the vision, leaders can inspire collective Action rooted in faith rather than external rewards. This approach ensures that the motivation for Action is genuine and spiritually grounded.

Encouragement as a Daily Practice

Encouragement should be a continuous and intentional effort. Nehemiah's ability to rally the elders of Jerusalem was not only due to his faith but also because he communicated effectively, demonstrating confidence in God's provision. Similarly, in our daily lives, we are called to support one another with words of faith and encouragement, helping others overcome obstacles and stay focused on God's purposes.

Practical ways to implement this include:

Sharing personal testimonies of God's faithfulness to inspire others.

Recognizing and affirming the efforts and contributions of those around you.

Reminding others of God's promises through Scripture and prayer.

Encouraging perseverance by emphasizing the eternal rewards that await those who remain steadfast.

Through these actions, you reflect Christ's love and foster a community where faith and hope thrive, much like Nehemiah did when rebuilding Jerusalem's walls.

Purpose and Benefits of Action Plans

The primary purpose of an action plan is to provide structure and clarity for achieving objectives. It ensures that all team members understand their roles, the tasks at hand, and the tools needed to succeed. Additionally, it offers a framework for resource allocation and performance tracking, enabling timely adjustments to stay on course.

Action plans offer several benefits, including:

Clarifying Objectives: A detailed plan prevents ambiguity, ensuring everyone understands the goal and their contributions.

Promoting Accountability: Assigning specific tasks fosters ownership and collective responsibility among team members.

Staying on Track: Deadlines and milestones help measure progress and maintain focus on the goal.

Measuring Success: Tracking performance against defined milestones provides insights into outcomes and areas for improvement.

Fostering Collaboration: Bringing together individuals with diverse skills and perspectives encourages innovation and shared commitment.

Encouraging Reflection: A well-documented plan provides opportunities to analyze what worked, what didn't, and how future projects can be improved.

Steps to Create an Effective Action Plan

Define SMART Goals: Clearly articulate what you aim to achieve, ensuring it is specific, measurable, achievable, relevant, and time-bound.

List Required Steps: Break the goal into smaller tasks, allowing for iterative refinement as new details emerge.

Prioritize and Set Deadlines: Organize tasks by importance and sequence, assigning realistic completion dates.

Establish Milestones: Identify intermediate goals that provide a sense of progress and maintain motivation.

Identify Resources: Ensure all necessary tools, skills, and resources are available or plan to acquire them.

Visualize Success: Create a mental or visual representation of achieving the goal to sustain motivation.

Review and Adjust: Regularly revisit the plan to ensure it remains relevant and realistic, making necessary adjustments based on progress and challenges.

By aligning action plans with their purpose—organizing tasks, fostering collaboration, and driving accountability—they become powerful tools for project success and personal growth. Whether managing a professional project or pursuing personal goals, a well-crafted action plan ensures clarity, structure, and measurable progress.

Overcoming Obstacles

Obstacles are the barriers that stand between you and your goals, acting as limiting factors that impede progress toward achieving your dreams. To advance in life and realize your aspirations, these hurdles must be confronted and overcome.

While setting goals is an essential first step, the real challenge lies in bringing those goals to fruition. The journey toward actualization often becomes daunting as unforeseen setbacks and obstacles emerge, testing your resolve and determination.

It is no exaggeration to state that success is inherently tied to challenges. These challenges typically present themselves as problems requiring resolution. By addressing and overcoming these difficulties, you build the confidence and resilience needed to pursue your objectives. Overcoming obstacles is a critical aspect of personal and professional growth, transforming challenges into opportunities to strengthen your capacity for success.

Relying on Philippians 4:13—"I can do all things through Christ who strengthens me"—offers profound comfort and encouragement when facing challenges or battling inner doubt. This verse emphasizes the boundless strength available through faith and a relationship with God, reminding believers that their abilities are not limited by personal capacity alone but are empowered by divine grace. Here's how it can be applied:

1. Acknowledging the Source of Strength

Philippians 4:13 shifts the focus from self-reliance to reliance on Christ. When inner doubt whispers inadequacy, this verse reinforces that the strength to overcome does not originate from our own power but from the limitless power of God. This dependence brings peace, knowing that we are not alone in our struggles.

2. Overcoming Fear and Weakness

Inner doubt often amplifies feelings of weakness or fear. By meditating on this Scripture, believers can find reassurance that God's strength compensates for human frailty. It encourages stepping forward in faith, trusting that God equips those He calls.

3. Cultivating a Positive Mindset

Philippians 4:13 reminds us that challenges are not insurmountable. Instead of succumbing to negative thoughts, believers can affirm this verse to replace doubt with faith, hope, and determination.

4. Encouragement in Adversity

This verse is especially relevant during tough times. Whether it's facing professional struggles, personal setbacks, or emotional battles, it assures us that Christ's strength is sufficient to sustain us, even in the most overwhelming situations.

5. Practical Steps to Apply the Verse

Pray for Strength: Regular prayer invites God's strength into specific challenges, reinforcing faith and reliance on Him.

Meditate on the Promise: Reflecting on this verse daily can serve as a powerful reminder of God's unwavering support.

Act in Faith: Take small steps toward your goals, trusting that God will provide the strength to succeed.

6. Finding Confidence in God's Purpose

Philippians 4:13 not only reassures us of strength but also highlights that God has a purpose for our lives. This perspective shifts our focus from self-doubt to trust in His plan, allowing us to move forward with confidence.

Relying on Philippians 4:13 transforms inner doubt into faith-filled Action. By anchoring our strength in Christ, we are reminded that no obstacle is too great and no challenge too overwhelming when God's power is at work in us.

Obstacles are an inevitable part of life, and overcoming them is vital for personal growth and achievement. It is impossible to navigate through life without encountering limitations, as challenges are inherent to the human experience. Rather than viewing obstacles as insurmountable barriers, they can be seen as opportunities for transformation and learning. Here are seven reasons why obstacles are crucial and how they contribute to personal and professional development:

1. Obstacles Reveal Your True Identity

Life's challenges can expose your strengths, limitations, and hidden potential. These moments of adversity push you to discover your resilience and capabilities. For instance, encountering setbacks in a new job or project can reveal your ability to adapt and persevere. By overcoming obstacles, you gain a clearer understanding of who you are and what you can achieve.

2. Obstacles Direct Your Actions

Challenges often redirect your focus and prompt you to find innovative solutions. They create opportunities to reassess priorities and adopt new strategies. For example, if someone continually tests your patience, it becomes an opportunity to cultivate forgiveness and emotional intelligence. Benjamin Franklin aptly stated, "The things which hurt, instruct." Obstacles guide you toward the lessons needed to progress in life.

3. Obstacles Build Resilience

No one is inherently equipped to face life's difficulties. Resilience is a skill developed through confronting and overcoming challenges. Each obstacle toughens you, preparing you for future hurdles. For example, managing financial difficulties might teach you the importance of budgeting and financial planning, making you more resourceful in the long run.

4. Obstacles Help You Focus on What Matters

When faced with challenges, it becomes essential to prioritize what truly counts. Clear goals make obstacles appear smaller and more manageable. Conversely, a lack of direction can magnify challenges, making them seem insurmountable. By focusing on your objectives and maintaining clarity, you can channel your energy toward meaningful pursuits.

5. Obstacles Unleash Creativity

Adversity often sparks creativity. When conventional approaches fail, obstacles force you to think outside the box. For instance, limited resources might lead you to discover innovative methods or strategies. Just as a lion in the jungle compels you to run faster, challenges drive you to tap into untapped potential and achieve extraordinary results.

6. Obstacles Provide Life with Meaning

The way you perceive and respond to obstacles shapes your life's narrative. Historical figures like Abraham Lincoln found profound meaning through their struggles. Lincoln's resilience during the Civil War exemplifies how adversity can inspire a higher purpose. By channeling challenges into meaningful actions, you can derive purpose and fulfillment.

7. Obstacles Encourage Compassion and Connection

Overcoming personal obstacles often fosters empathy for others. By shifting your focus outward, you not only lift others but also gain a renewed perspective on your own challenges. Helping others navigate their struggles can be a powerful way to find meaning and rise above your own limitations.

7 Ways to Overcome Obstacles in Life

Identify Limiting Factors

Begin by assessing what is hindering you from reaching your goals. Instead of blaming external circumstances, identify areas you can control, such as procrastination, complacency, or poor planning.

Review the Timeline of the Obstacle

Reflect on how long the challenge has persisted and the habits or attitudes contributing to it. This insight can help you make the necessary adjustments to overcome it.

Focus on What You Can Control

Some obstacles are beyond your control, but you can still influence your response. Cultivate good habits, make better decisions, and prioritize self-care to maintain a positive outlook.

Break Goals into Smaller Steps

Large goals can seem overwhelming. Breaking them into smaller, actionable steps makes them more achievable. For instance, enrolling in a course or dedicating time daily to skill development can propel you toward larger aspirations.

Maintain an Active Plan

Work with a to-do list that acknowledges potential obstacles. Flexibility in your plan allows you to adapt to challenges and find alternative strategies to achieve your goals.

Enhance Problem-Solving Skills

Instead of relying solely on instinct, adopt a more analytical approach to decision-making. Evaluate problems logically and seek creative solutions.

By embracing obstacles as opportunities for growth, you can transform setbacks into stepping stones toward a fulfilling and meaningful life.

The story of David and Goliath is a profound example of how courage, faith, and resourcefulness can overcome fear and seemingly insurmountable challenges. Drawing from this biblical narrative, here's how the lessons from David's triumph can help address fears:

1. Acknowledge Your Fears Without Letting Them Paralyze You

The Israelite army was paralyzed with fear at the sight of Goliath, an imposing and seemingly unbeatable giant. David, a young shepherd, faced the same intimidating reality, but he refused to be overwhelmed by fear. Instead, he acknowledged the challenge and stepped forward with confidence in his abilities and faith in a higher power.

Application: Recognize your fears for what they are—natural responses to perceived threats. However, do not let them immobilize you. Instead, channel your energy into Action, focusing on what you can control.

2. Draw Strength from Past Victories

When King Saul questioned David's ability to fight Goliath, David recounted how he had previously defended his sheep by defeating a lion and a bear. These past victories gave him the confidence to face an even greater challenge.

Application: Reflect on your own experiences where you've successfully overcome difficulties. These moments serve as evidence of your resilience and can give you the courage to face new challenges.

3. Face the Challenge with the Right Tools

Goliath came armed with heavy weapons and armor, while David carried only a sling and five smooth stones. Rather than engaging Goliath on his terms, David used the tools he was familiar with—tools that matched his strengths.

Application: Don't try to confront your fears using methods or strategies that don't align with your abilities or values. Instead, leverage your unique strengths and resources to address challenges in a way that feels authentic to you.

4. Have Faith in a Higher Purpose

David's faith in God was unshakable. He believed that his battle against Goliath was not just about him but about defending the honor of his people and his faith. This conviction gave him the courage to face Goliath without hesitation.

Application: Connecting your actions to a greater purpose can help diminish fear. Whether it's faith, a sense of duty, or a personal mission, focusing on the bigger picture can give you the strength to persevere.

5. Understand That Giants Can Be Defeated

To the Israelites, Goliath seemed invincible. But David saw him as vulnerable—a mortal being who could be brought down with a well-placed stone. His perspective shifted the narrative from "impossible" to "achievable."

Application: Fear often magnifies challenges, making them seem larger than they are. Reframe the situation to focus on solutions rather than obstacles. Break down the "giant" into smaller, manageable parts, and you'll see that even the biggest challenges can be overcome.

6. Act Despite Fear

David could have easily retreated like the rest of the Israelites, but he chose to act. His courage wasn't the absence of fear but his determination to move forward despite it.

Application: Courage is not about erasing fear but about refusing to let it dictate your actions. Take the first step, no matter how small, and let momentum carry you forward.

7. Victory Comes Through Determination, Not Size or Power

David's triumph over Goliath wasn't because he matched Goliath's physical might but because he outsmarted him with strategy, precision, and faith. His story proves that even the smallest and seemingly least prepared can achieve great victories through determination and creativity.

Application: Remind yourself that you don't need to be the strongest or most equipped to overcome challenges. By focusing on your strengths, having faith in your abilities, and acting with determination, you can overcome fears and emerge victorious.

In essence, the story of David and Goliath teaches us that fear is natural, but it can be overcome with courage, faith, and the right mindset. Facing your "giants" head-on, armed with your unique abilities and purpose, can lead to transformative victories in life.

Battling Inner Doubt

Battling inner doubt is a journey many of us face, whether in personal endeavors or professional aspirations. Inner doubt, often fueled by fear of failure, comparison, or past experiences, can be a significant barrier to growth and achievement. However, there are strategies to overcome this and build confidence.

1. Identify the Root Cause

Understanding the origin of your doubt is crucial. Ask yourself questions like:

What specific situations trigger these feelings?

Are these doubts rooted in past failures or external pressures?

For example, if you're stepping into a new role or launching a new project, the unknown can amplify doubt. Recognizing this allows you to focus on actionable solutions rather than being paralyzed by fear.

2. Challenge Negative Thoughts

Our inner critic often magnifies fears and minimizes achievements. Combat this by:

Writing down self-doubt thoughts and rephrasing them into positive affirmations.

Reflecting on past successes, no matter how small, to remind yourself of your capabilities.

3. Set Realistic Goals

Doubt can stem from setting unattainable standards. Break larger goals into smaller, achievable milestones. Celebrating small victories builds momentum and reinforces self-belief.

4. Seek Support

Share your feelings with trusted friends, mentors, or colleagues. They can offer perspective, encouragement, and constructive feedback. Sometimes, hearing someone else's confidence in you can be transformative.

5. Practice Self-Compassion

Treat yourself with kindness. Acknowledge that doubt is a natural part of growth, and mistakes are opportunities to learn. Embrace imperfections and focus on progress, not perfection.

6. Take Action

Inaction can fuel doubt. Start small, even if you're unsure. Each step forward builds confidence and reduces the grip of self-doubt. For example, if you doubt your skills in a professional setting, volunteering for a small task can prove to yourself and others that you're capable.

7. Focus on Growth

Shift your mindset from "What if I fail?" to "What can I learn?" A growth-oriented mindset allows you to view challenges as opportunities for improvement rather than as threats.

8. Limit Comparisons

Comparing yourself to others often worsens self-doubt. Remember, everyone is on a unique journey. Focus on your progress and strengths.

9. Professional Help

If inner doubt persists and affects your well-being, consider seeking help from a coach, therapist, or counselor. They can provide tools and techniques to manage these feelings effectively.

Battling inner doubt is an ongoing process that requires self-awareness, persistence, and the willingness to take risks. Over time, these efforts cultivate resilience, empowering you to face challenges with confidence and optimism.

Turning Setbacks into Stepping Stones

Life's most meaningful achievements often stem from our capacity to face challenges head-on rather than avoiding them. While setbacks can feel discouraging, they are not insurmountable roadblocks. Instead, they serve as disguised lessons, shaping us into more resilient and adaptable individuals. For high achievers who place great value on results and excellence, setbacks can feel like personal failures—but this perspective can be transformed.

Matt Clark, a firefighter and coach, exemplifies how adversity builds resilience. Through experiences leading teams in life-or-death scenarios and coaching clients to unlock their potential, he emphasizes the philosophy of "Progress, Not Perfection." This approach highlights that growth emerges not from flawless execution but from consistent, intentional effort—even when failure is part of the journey.

If you've ever felt immobilized by past mistakes or doubted your ability to recover from setbacks, it's time to shift your perspective. By viewing setbacks as opportunities for growth rather than as failures, you can transform obstacles into stepping stones that propel you forward.

Why Do Setbacks Feel So Overwhelming?

For high performers, setbacks can trigger a cascade of negative emotions, primarily frustration and self-doubt. This reaction often stems from societal conditioning that equates success with perfection. When immediate results don't materialize, it's easy to feel defeated and question your capabilities.

When setbacks occur, the inner critic often takes over with thoughts like, "How did I not see this coming?" or "Am I even capable of succeeding?" This mindset can lead to analysis paralysis—reliving missteps instead of focusing on solutions. For those who tie their self-worth to performance, one setback can feel like a blow to their entire identity, creating a fear of failure that stalls progress altogether.

The truth is that setbacks are inevitable. The key lies not in avoiding them but in handling them with purpose and resilience.

Setbacks as Catalysts for Growth

Life's most fulfilling achievements often arise not from avoiding challenges but from navigating them with courage and faith. Setbacks, while uncomfortable, are not roadblocks but opportunities in disguise, shaping us into stronger, more adaptable individuals. This principle resonates profoundly in the story of Joseph from the Bible, whose journey exemplifies resilience and growth amidst adversity.

Joseph, sold into slavery by his brothers, endured betrayal, false accusations, and imprisonment. Yet, he remained steadfast in his faith, trusting that God was working through his trials for a greater purpose. Reflecting on his hardships, Joseph proclaimed in Genesis 50:20: "You intended to harm me, but God intended it for good to accomplish what is now being done, the saving of many lives." This declaration reminds us that setbacks can be divinely repurposed into stepping stones for growth and triumph.

Why Setbacks Feel So Heavy

For many, setbacks trigger frustration and self-doubt, particularly for high achievers who often tie their worth to performance. Like Joseph, we may question our circumstances and wonder why challenges arise. When Joseph was thrown into a pit by his brothers and later imprisoned unjustly, it would have been easy for him to succumb to despair. However, his story illustrates that the weight of a setback often lies in our perception of it and in our ability to trust the Process.

The Real Struggle

Joseph's journey reveals the danger of allowing setbacks to paralyze us. When our inner critic dominates, we replay our missteps and allow fear to overshadow faith. Joseph's ability to rise above betrayal and injustice showcases the power of resilience rooted in trust—in God, in purpose, and in the redemptive potential of challenges. For high achievers, this mindset can be transformative. It shifts focus from perfection to progress, encouraging us to embrace adversity as part of the journey rather than a reflection of our worth.

The Opportunity in Setbacks

Setbacks are fertile ground for growth. Just as Joseph's trials prepared him to govern Egypt and save countless lives, our challenges refine our character, build our resilience, and equip us for future opportunities. Every misstep teaches us valuable lessons and strengthens our ability to adapt. Joseph's story underscores that no setback is wasted when we remain open to learning and growth.

Turning Setbacks into Stepping Stones

Joseph's life offers a blueprint for transforming setbacks into growth opportunities, much like the following practical strategies:

Reframe Setbacks as Learning Opportunities

Joseph's resilience stemmed from his ability to view hardships through a lens of faith and purpose. Sold into slavery, he adapted and excelled in Potiphar's house. Imprisoned unjustly, he found favor by interpreting dreams. In each instance, Joseph recognized the opportunity to grow despite his circumstances.

🔑 Action Step: Reflect on a recent setback. Write down what happened, what you learned, and how it might be preparing you for a greater purpose.

Break Down the Big Picture

Joseph's journey was long and filled with obstacles, yet he remained faithful to God's vision for his life. Rather than becoming overwhelmed, he focused on excelling in the roles presented to him, one step at a time.

🔑 Action Step: Identify one small step you can take toward your goal today, even if the ultimate destination feels distant.

Build Resilience Through Consistent Faith and Habits

Joseph's unshakable faith in God and his consistent efforts, even in dire circumstances, demonstrate how daily habits and trust in a higher plan can build resilience.

🔑 Action Step: Strengthen a daily habit that nurtures your faith or personal growth, such as prayer, gratitude journaling, or acts of service.

Celebrate Progress, Not Just Results

Joseph's ultimate success wasn't immediate, but each small victory—gaining trust, interpreting dreams, being elevated to positions of authority—was a step toward his destiny. Recognizing these moments reinforced his resilience and commitment.

🔑 Action Step: At the end of each week, list three achievements, big or small, that reflect your progress toward your goals.

Reflection & Next Steps

Joseph's journey reminds us that setbacks are not the end of the story; they are pivotal chapters in a greater narrative. His faith in God's plan enabled him to rise above adversity and fulfill his purpose. Like Joseph, we can embrace setbacks as opportunities to realign, refocus, and grow stronger.

Take a moment to reflect:

What's one area of your life where you can trust the Process and embrace progress over perfection?

How can you reframe a recent setback to see the growth it offers?

Remember, resilience isn't about avoiding failure but about trusting that every challenge serves a purpose. Joseph's story shows us that what others intend for harm; God can use for good. Each setback is a stepping stone, each small step is progress, and each lesson learned is a victory paving the way for success.

Setbacks, while uncomfortable, are essential for personal development. Just as muscles grow stronger through resistance, your resilience develops when challenged. Each setback offers a chance to adapt, refine strategies, and move forward with renewed clarity.

Consider how failures have fueled some of history's greatest success stories. Thomas Edison, for instance, famously reframed his failed experiments as steps toward innovation, stating, "I have not failed. I've just found 10,000 ways that won't work." By adopting a mindset that sees setbacks as opportunities, you can cultivate growth and transformation.

Strategies for Turning Setbacks into Stepping Stones

1. Reframe Setbacks as Opportunities for Learning

Rather than viewing setbacks as failures, treat them as feedback that redirects you to a better path. Each challenge provides insight into what works and what doesn't.

Example:

Imagine you've prepared extensively for a presentation that falls flat. Instead of dwelling on what went wrong, reflect on the feedback. Perhaps simplifying your message or practicing delivery could enhance your impact.

Action Step:

Reflect on a recent setback. Ask yourself:

What happened?

What did I learn?

How can I apply this lesson to future efforts?

This shift from self-criticism to self-improvement lays the foundation for progress.

2. Break Down Goals into Manageable Steps

Setbacks often feel overwhelming because they make long-term goals seem unattainable. Focusing on incremental progress, rather than the bigger picture, can make challenges feel less daunting.

Example:

If you're training for a marathon and suffer an injury, don't give up. Focus on recovery, set smaller milestones, and gradually rebuild your strength.

Action Step:

Choose one small, achievable goal each day. For example:

Overwhelmed at work? Focus on completing one priority task.

Struggling with fitness? Commit to a short walk or stretch session.

Each small win builds momentum and keeps you moving forward.

3. Cultivate Resilience Through Consistent Habits

Resilience isn't innate—it's a skill you can build through daily practice. Simple habits like journaling, meditation, or regular exercise strengthen your ability to navigate challenges with clarity and emotional stability.

Example:

Start a gratitude journal or dedicate 10 minutes daily to reflect on what went well. These habits create a mental foundation, making setbacks easier to navigate.

Action Step:

Select one habit to prioritize this week, such as:

Write three things you're grateful for.

Spending time reflecting on positive experiences.

Consistency is key. Over time, these practices become your safety net during tough times.

4. Celebrate Progress, Not Just Results

High achievers often overlook small victories, focusing only on long-term outcomes. However, celebrating progress—even incremental steps—reinforces motivation and a growth mindset.

Example:

If you're writing a book, don't wait until it's finished to celebrate. Acknowledge milestones like drafting chapters or refining key ideas.

Action Step:

At the end of each week, write down three accomplishments, no matter how small. Reflect on how they contribute to your overarching goals.

Reflection: Building Your Path Forward

Setbacks are not the end of the road—they're opportunities to realign, grow, and move closer to your goals. By embracing progress over perfection, you allow yourself to focus on the journey, not just the destination.

Take a moment to reflect:

What's one area in your life where you can embrace progress over perfection?

What small step can you take today to move forward?

If a recent setback is holding you back, let it guide—not define—you. Ask yourself: What can I learn from this? How can it make me stronger?

Resilience is not about avoiding failure; it's about rising stronger after every fall. By transforming setbacks into stepping stones, you'll not only achieve success but also unlock your true potential.

The Parable of the Talents (Matthew 25:14-30) provides a powerful lesson on responsibility, stewardship, and the necessity of overcoming the fear of failure. It tells the story of a master who entrusts his servants with varying amounts of talents (a form of currency) according to their abilities before leaving on a journey. When he returns, the master finds that two of the servants have wisely invested and multiplied their talents, while the third buries him in fear, gaining nothing. This parable highlights the consequences of both faith-driven Action and fear-driven inaction.

The Fear of Failure in the Parable

The third servant's response illustrates how fear of failure can lead to stagnation. When asked to account for his talent, he admits:

"I was afraid, and I went and hid your talent in the ground" (Matthew 25:25).

His fear of losing the master's money paralyzed him, causing him to squander an opportunity for growth. This response reflects a mindset many individuals struggle with—one where fear of making mistakes or disappointing others prevents them from taking risks or stepping into their full potential.

For high achievers and those striving for excellence, this fear can be particularly potent. Like the servant, they may bury their talents, choosing safety over the uncertainty that comes with Action, only to miss out on opportunities to grow and make an impact.

Lessons on Overcoming Fear of Failure

Recognizing That Fear is Paralyzing, Not Protective

The servant's fear led him to hide his talent, accomplishing nothing for himself or his master. Similarly, when we let fear dominate, it keeps us from trying, growing, and contributing. The other servants, who acted boldly, not only multiplied their talents but also received the master's commendation:

"Well done, good and faithful servant! You have been faithful with a few things; I will put you in charge of many things" (Matthew 25:21).

This demonstrates that faith and effort, even with inherent risks, yield rewards far greater than the comfort of inaction.

Embracing Responsibility and Faith

The parable underscores the importance of trust—both in God's provision and in our abilities as stewards of His gifts. Each servant was given talents "according to his ability" (Matthew 25:15), signifying that the master had confidence in them. Similarly, God equips each of us with unique skills, resources, and opportunities. Focusing on faithful effort rather than fearing potential failure honors that trust.

Viewing Effort as Worship

Using our talents is an act of worship and a way to glorify God. Whether our "talents" are literal resources, skills, or opportunities, we are called to invest them wisely. Hiding our abilities out of fear dishonors their purpose and deprives both ourselves and others of their benefits. The two faithful servants serve as reminders that Action—guided by faith—is more pleasing to God than inaction rooted in fear.

Accepting That Failure Can Lead to Growth

The master did not demand perfection, only faithfulness. Even if the servant had risked the talent and lost it, his effort might have been commended. This reflects a key truth: failure, when approached with the right mindset, becomes a stepping stone for growth and wisdom. Fear of failure often magnifies its risks while minimizing the growth and learning that can result from trying.

Application in Overcoming Fear of Failure

Shift Your Perspective on Risk

Instead of viewing risk as something to fear, see it as an opportunity for growth. Like the faithful servants, consider how acting boldly with your "talents" can lead to greater possibilities and impact.

Take Small, Faithful Steps

Overcoming fear doesn't require giant leaps. Begin with small acts of faith and effort, gradually building confidence in your ability to manage challenges.

Trust in God's Plan

Recognize that God equips you with the resources and abilities needed for your journey. Faithfulness, not perfection, is the goal. Trust that He can use even your mistakes for good.

Celebrate Progress, Not Just Outcomes

Like the master commending his faithful servants, focus on effort and growth rather than just results. This mindset allows you to appreciate the journey, not just the destination.

Reflection

The Parable of the Talents challenges us to confront the fear of failure and embrace the responsibility of stewarding our gifts wisely. Take a moment to reflect:

What talents or opportunities has God entrusted to you?

Are there areas where fear is holding you back from acting faithfully?

Remember, the measure of success in God's eyes is not perfection but faithfulness and willingness to try. Step boldly, invest your talents, and trust that God will bless your efforts for His glory.

Perseverance in Purpose

Perseverance is the capacity to steadfastly pursue goals or passions over time, even when faced with setbacks or challenges. The Values in Action Inventory of Strengths defines perseverance as "finishing what one starts; persevering in the course of action despite obstacles; 'getting it out the door'; taking pleasure in completing tasks." This attribute is interlinked with resilience, motivation, grit, and conscientiousness, all of which serve as pillars for sustained effort and determination (Duckworth, 2016).

Research consistently demonstrates that perseverance surpasses innate talent as a predictor of success (Duckworth et al., 2007). The ability to persist entails more than effort; it encompasses the willingness to learn from failure, embrace discomfort, and try repeatedly until obstacles are overcome (Dweck, 2017). This quality aligns closely with purpose, as both involve a commitment to long-term objectives and a drive to create meaningful impact.

Perseverance plays a pivotal role in deepening faith and leading to breakthroughs, as it allows individuals to endure challenges, trust in a higher purpose, and grow stronger through trials. This transformative Process intertwines the spiritual, emotional, and cognitive aspects of human resilience.

Perseverance as a Test of Faith

Faith often requires trust in outcomes that are not immediately visible or guaranteed. When faced with adversity, perseverance becomes how individuals maintain belief in their goals or divine purpose despite external circumstances. As stated in James 1:3-4, "the testing of your faith produces perseverance. Let perseverance finish its work so that you may be mature and complete, not lacking anything." Here, perseverance is depicted as the path to spiritual maturity, requiring patience and endurance to align one's actions with one's faith.

Building Trust and Patience

Perseverance strengthens faith by teaching individuals to trust the Process, even when immediate results are not evident. For instance, in times of uncertainty or failure, people are often encouraged to lean into their spiritual beliefs for guidance and solace. This trust fosters patience, a virtue deeply connected with spiritual growth. By continuing to work toward a breakthrough while surrendering the outcome to a higher power, individuals cultivate a deeper sense of reliance and humility.

Spiritual Growth Through Struggle

Difficulties are often the crucible for spiritual and personal breakthroughs. Perseverance through trials provides an opportunity for reflection, self-improvement, and renewed faith. For example, enduring hardships can reveal hidden strengths, clarify one's purpose, and foster gratitude for incremental progress. The biblical story of Job is a testament to this, as Job's unwavering perseverance through immense suffering ultimately led to restoration and blessings beyond his initial circumstances (Job 42:10).

Leading to Breakthroughs

Breakthroughs often emerge when perseverance intersects with divine timing or the culmination of consistent effort. This Process is not just about enduring but about active engagement—continuing to pray, act, learn, and trust even when progress seems slow. Breakthroughs can be seen as both external (achieving goals) and internal (developing qualities such as faith, patience, and resilience).

For example, in personal struggles such as overcoming addiction, rebuilding relationships, or pursuing long-term goals, perseverance enables individuals to grow through each failure, learning and adapting until success is achieved. This persistence not only achieves the desired outcome but also reinforces faith in oneself and the Process.

The Role of Hope in Perseverance

Hope is the driving force behind perseverance, particularly in faith. It sustains the belief that circumstances can improve and that effort will yield results. As Angela Duckworth (2016) notes in her studies on grit, hope is a critical component of perseverance. In the context of faith, this hope is often rooted in trust in divine providence or the belief in a greater plan.

Reflection Questions

How does my current vision align with my faith and personal growth goals?

What intentional actions can I take today to move closer to my God-centered vision?

What obstacles or fears are holding me back, and how can I reframe them as opportunities for growth?

How can I practice daily encouragement to stay aligned with my purpose?

Action Steps

Write It Down: Draft a clear vision statement that integrates your spiritual values and life goals. Revisit it regularly.

Clarify Goals: Break your vision into achievable, intentional steps with timelines to maintain focus and momentum.

Overcome Setbacks: When faced with obstacles, reflect on lessons learned and adopt strategies to turn setbacks into stepping stones.

Celebrate Progress: Acknowledge small wins along the journey to sustain motivation and reinforce perseverance.

Chapter Four
The Power of Relationships

Relationships are fundamental to the human experience, profoundly shaping our lives. They imbue our lives with meaning and purpose through romantic partnerships, friendships, familial bonds, or professional connections. However, developing deep, fulfilling connections requires awareness, effort, and skills that many of us must consciously cultivate. This guide explores relationships' vital role in our well-being and provides actionable strategies to enhance the ones most matter.

Why Relationships Matter

Our connections with others are crucial to our emotional and physical health, success, and longevity. Relationships fulfill a deeply rooted evolutionary need for social bonds. Humans have thrived as communal beings through affection, protection, and cooperative living for millennia. These bonds have been pivotal in personal growth and societal progress.

When we view our personal growth, we often imagine a solitary journey, navigating a roadmap toward self-improvement. However, relationships are the true compass, helping us make critical turns in our growth journey. Whether pursuing personal or leadership development goals, our connections are essential allies in our quest for success.

The Role of Relationships in Personal Growth

The C.L.E.A.R. framework by Maxwell Leadership® emphasizes that relationships are an integral "growth lane" in achieving personal and professional aspirations. While individual responsibility is the cornerstone of growth, relationships serve as catalysts, amplifying our progress. As John C. Maxwell and Traci Morrow highlight, if we aim to add value to the world, we must first recognize and embrace the value others bring to our lives.

Four Key Ways Relationships Foster Growth

Expertise

Relationships provide access to valuable insights from those who have walked the path before us. Mentors, guides, and experienced peers offer wisdom and perspectives that shape our decision-making and help us navigate challenges.

Encouragement

During difficult moments, the support of others keeps us motivated and focused. Relationships remind us of our goals, ensuring we do not lose heart when faced with adversity.

Accountability

Trusted connections serve as checkpoints, holding us accountable for our progress. They ensure we remain aligned with our objectives and maintain momentum toward our aspirations.

Celebration

Recognizing milestones and achievements is an essential aspect of growth. Relationships provide the joy of shared victories, helping us appreciate how far we've come and inspiring us to reach further.

Whether a single person fulfills all these roles or a network of individuals contributes uniquely, relationships are indispensable for personal development.

Harnessing the Power of Relationships

The power of relationships lies in their ability to influence our growth positively. By connecting with others meaningfully, we enrich our lives and unlock the potential to achieve our most ambitious goals. When we allow relationships to guide, support, and celebrate us, we foster a culture of mutual growth and empowerment.

The teachings of John C. Maxwell and the principles of the C.L.E.A.R. framework provide a roadmap for leveraging relationships in our growth journey. By actively engaging with the people around us, we can transform our lives and create a legacy of meaningful connections and shared success.

Building a Support Network

We often lean on our support systems during difficult times—friends, family, coworkers, community members, or healthcare professionals like therapists. These connections form a safety net that provides comfort, advice, and practical help. However, life changes, increasing reliance on digital communication, and the physical distancing experienced during recent years can all influence the size and strength of our support networks, directly affecting our mental health and resilience.

What is a Support System?

A support system is a network of individuals who offer emotional, mental, or practical help when needed. This could involve listening to your concerns, providing encouragement, or offering hands-on assistance, like help with finances or childcare. Support systems also play a vital role during good times, sustaining momentum and reinforcing confidence.

A strong support system is not a sign of weakness; it enhances problem-solving abilities and fosters resilience by bolstering autonomy, confidence, and self-esteem. It's about receiving help, giving back, and creating reciprocal, mutually beneficial relationships.

The Importance of a Support System

The isolation and reduced social support experienced during the pandemic underscored the importance of a robust support network. According to the American Psychological Association's Stress in America survey (2022), more than half of respondents wished they had received more emotional support during that time. A lack of social connections is associated with significant health issues, including high blood pressure, weakened immunity, cardiovascular disease, and cognitive decline. Low social support is linked to increased risks of death from cardiovascular diseases, infectious diseases, and cancer.

On the other hand, strong support systems reduce stress, enhance emotional well-being, and improve physical health, resilience, and overall life satisfaction.

What Makes a Strong Support System?

Effective support systems are characterized by individuals who genuinely care about you, offer stability, and show compassion. Equally, relationships should be reciprocal—you support others just as they support you. Taking stock of your current support system can help identify gaps, reveal hesitation patterns to seek help, and clarify how others can better support you.

Building a Support Network

Creating or strengthening a support system takes intention and effort. Here are some strategies:

Define Your Needs

Reflect on what you need from your support network. Are you seeking emotional support, professional advice, or companionship? Knowing your priorities will guide you in finding the right people to meet these needs.

Expand Beyond the Familiar

While friends and family are valuable, broadening your network to include coworkers, neighbors, or online communities can increase the diversity of perspectives and resources available to you. This variety makes you more likely to find someone with the skills and understanding to meet specific needs.

Nurture Relationships

Regularly investing time and effort into existing relationships strengthens bonds. Be proactive in contacting friends or acquaintances, even if it's a simple check-in message or a shared activity. Building habits, like dedicating an hour each week to connect with others, ensure these efforts are sustained.

Engage in Shared Interests

Joining hobby groups, volunteering, or attending community events can help you meet like-minded individuals. Whether it's a book club, exercise class, or online forum, shared passions often lead to meaningful and lasting connections.

Seek Professional Support

Therapists, counselors, and healthcare providers are valuable support network members. They offer unbiased guidance and tools to navigate challenges. They provide a unique perspective that complements personal relationships.

Balance Giving and Receiving

Strong support networks thrive on mutual effort. Studies suggest that offering support to others can be as beneficial as receiving it. Checking in, showing appreciation, and being available when others need help build trust and deepen connections.

Overcoming Challenges in Building a Support System

Growing a network comes with challenges like vulnerability, time, or finding the right fit. Opening up to new people can feel intimidating, and it may take patience to form meaningful connections. Additionally, it's essential to recognize when certain relationships no longer serve your well-being and adjust accordingly.

Relating It All to Mental Health

A robust support network serves as a cornerstone for mental health. By surrounding yourself with diverse and caring individuals, you enhance your ability to cope with stress, navigate life's uncertainties, and celebrate successes. Equally important is self-support—practicing self-care, developing coping mechanisms, and setting boundaries ensures you remain resilient and independent even as you rely on others.

Ultimately, building a strong support system requires a combination of introspection, proactive effort, and mutual respect. Whether you start by strengthening existing relationships or venturing into new social spaces, each step contributes to a network that can sustain and uplift you through all stages of life.

The importance of community in personal and spiritual growth.

Community provides an essential foundation for personal and spiritual growth by fostering a sense of belonging, shared purpose, and mutual support. We feel validated and understood when surrounded by individuals who share similar interests, values, or beliefs. This sense of belonging creates a supportive environment where we can express ourselves without fear of judgment, encouraging authenticity and self-acceptance. As Dr. Roger Patterson reflects, "What would your life be like if, in your Christian community and your group, the people in your life loved you despite your flaws? That would be a place you would want to keep going." Such acceptance is pivotal for growth, as it nurtures a safe space to confront our imperfections and strive for betterment.

Shared Goals and Purpose

Being part of a community aligns individuals toward common goals, instilling a sense of fulfillment and Collaboration. For example, a church congregation working to make a positive impact or a sports team striving for victory demonstrates the power of shared objectives. These collective efforts foster cooperation and a sense of contribution to something greater than oneself, which is inherently rewarding and motivating. For spiritual growth, shared rituals and communal activities help anchor individuals to shared beliefs while deepening their understanding of their faith.

Support and Encouragement

The community provides a vital support system in both joyous and challenging times. When faced with adversity, having people who genuinely care about your well-being offers reassurance and guidance, helping you navigate life's hurdles with resilience. Conversely, during moments of success, the encouragement of a community amplifies joy and gratitude. This emotional reinforcement strengthens interpersonal bonds and deepens one's spiritual journey, as shared experiences create profound connections and understanding.

Learning and Growth Through Diversity

Communities are fertile grounds for learning and personal growth, enriched by the diversity of perspectives and experiences within them. Engaging with others through discussions, mentorship, and shared activities broadens one's worldview, fostering empathy and understanding. Whether through a religious organization or a non-religious spiritual group, these interactions challenge preconceived notions, encouraging introspection and continuous learning. For example, meditation circles or retreat centers offer unique opportunities to learn new practices to enhance personal and spiritual well-being.

Unity and Overcoming Differences

Strong communities thrive on unity, which often requires navigating and reconciling differences. Acceptance, forgiveness, and a focus on shared values enable individuals to find common ground, even amidst diversity. By embracing imperfections and extending grace, communities foster an environment of empathy and resilience. For instance, in a spiritual context, navigating differences in belief with openness and curiosity can deepen understanding and strengthen relationships, promoting a culture of mutual respect and trust.

Building Healthy Community Relationships

Healthy relationships within a community are built on trust, respect, and genuine care. Open communication fosters transparency and understanding, while conflict resolution encourages healing and growth. For example, viewing disagreements as opportunities for dialogue rather than barriers can strengthen community bonds and reaffirm shared goals. Moreover, group rituals and practices, such as collective meditation or prayer, reinforce these connections by creating shared experiences that deepen emotional and spiritual ties.

Addressing Challenges in Community Spirituality

While the community offers numerous benefits, it also presents challenges, particularly in navigating diversity and differences in belief. Building inclusive environments requires intentional efforts to ensure everyone feels valued and heard. Open communication, empathy, and a willingness to engage with varying perspectives are vital to overcoming these hurdles. By fostering dialogue and celebrating diversity, communities can create spaces where individuals feel safe to explore their spiritual journeys without fear of judgment.

Cultivating Community in Everyday Life

To fully benefit from the power of community, it is essential to actively participate and seek out like-minded groups that align with your values and passions. Engage in activities, attend events, and contribute to the growth and well-being of the community. Open communication and empathy are key to nurturing meaningful relationships while celebrating diversity, which ensures an inclusive and supportive environment. Spiritual communities, whether religious or non-religious, offer opportunities for shared learning, personal growth, and exploring deeper meanings in life.

The Transformative Role of Community in Growth

Ultimately, community catalyzes personal and spiritual growth, providing the support, guidance, and shared experiences necessary for transformation. By embracing the unity and diversity within a community, we create spaces that empower individuals to grow, learn, and thrive. As we invest in these relationships and actively participate in communal life, we not only enhance our spiritual journey but also contribute to the collective strength and resilience of the community.

Choosing Your Circle

Humans are naturally social creatures, and the people we surround ourselves with play a critical role in shaping our thoughts, emotions, and actions. Our inner circle—composed of close friends, family, and colleagues—can either elevate us or hinder our growth. Here's why the people in your inner circle are so influential:

The Impact of Your Inner Circle

Emotional Support: During difficult times, having empathetic individuals in your circle can provide comfort and help you navigate challenges more effectively.

Motivation and Inspiration: Positive, ambitious people can inspire you to aim higher, set ambitious goals, and stay motivated through their achievements and outlook on life.

Accountability: A strong network keeps you accountable for your goals and reminds you of your potential, especially when you're tempted to quit.

Feedback and Growth: Constructive criticism from trusted individuals is invaluable for personal and professional development. Their honest insights foster self-improvement.

Scientific Insights on Social Influence

Research highlights the profound ways social connections shape our lives:

Social Contagion

Behavioral Contagion: Studies from Harvard Medical School and the University of California, San Diego, reveal that those around us influence behaviors like smoking, eating habits, and exercise. This "social contagion" means habits within your network can become your own.

Emotional Contagion: Research published in Psychological Science shows that emotions spread through social networks. Spending time with happy individuals can enhance your happiness, while exposure to negativity can increase stress and sadness.

Mental Health Impact

Stress and Anxiety: Strong social relationships reduce stress levels and the likelihood of depression, according to a study in the American Journal of Psychiatry.

Cognitive and Creative Benefits

Cognitive Decline: Studies in Neurology associate supportive networks with reduced risks of cognitive decline and dementia.

Problem-Solving: Research from the University of Michigan shows that diverse perspectives within your social circle enhance creativity and cognitive flexibility.

Professional Success

Career Growth: The Journal of Applied Psychology says strong professional networks boost career advancement and job satisfaction.

Work Productivity: MIT research links positive team dynamics with greater productivity and job engagement.

Identifying Positive Influences

Choosing the right people starts with seeking individuals who uplift and empower you. Look for these traits:

Positivity: Their optimism helps you maintain a constructive mindset.

Supportiveness: Genuine encouragement for your goals is key.

Integrity: Trustworthy, reliable individuals foster strong relationships.

Growth-Oriented: People committed to self-improvement inspire you to grow.

Letting Go of Negative Influences

Recognizing and distancing yourself from negative influences is equally vital:

Negativity: Persistent pessimism can drain your energy and affect your outlook.

Lack of Support: Those who belittle your dreams can hinder progress.

Dishonesty: Trust is foundational, and repeated betrayal necessitates boundaries.

Toxic Behaviors: Manipulative or critical individuals harm your mental well-being.

Building a Supportive Network

Once you've identified positive influences and distanced yourself from negative ones, focus on cultivating an empowering circle:

Connect with Like-Minded People: Join communities that share your interests and values, whether professional groups or online platforms.

Be Authentic: Open and honest relationships foster mutual trust and understanding.

Offer Support: Strengthen bonds by helping others, creating reciprocity and deeper connections.

Prioritize Relationships: Meaningful connections require time and consistent effort to flourish.

"Choosing Your Circle" underscores the importance of intentionally surrounding yourself with individuals who enhance your growth and well-being. By recognizing the profound influence of social connections on emotional resilience, mental health, cognitive function, and professional success, you can create an environment that aligns with your aspirations and values.

The decision about who you surround yourself with goes beyond avoiding toxic influences or seeking out successful individuals. It's about intentionally aligning your relationships with your values and long-term vision. Drawing inspiration from Warren Buffett's philosophy, here are key principles to consider:

1. Prioritize Character

Buffett emphasizes that Character outweighs intelligence or skill. People who demonstrate honesty, integrity, and reliability bring Positivity and stability to your life. These traits foster trust and mutual respect, essential for meaningful relationships.

2. Embrace Growth-Minded Individuals

Surround yourself with people who are committed to continual learning and self-improvement. These individuals inspire you to pursue your growth and create an environment where progress is celebrated and encouraged.

3. Seek Diverse Perspectives

A circle that challenges your thinking and broadens your viewpoint is invaluable. Engaging with individuals who offer different perspectives fosters critical thinking and innovative problem-solving, helping you grow in ways that a homogenous group cannot.

4. Focus on Mutually Beneficial Relationships

Healthy relationships are a two-way street. Invest in connections where both parties contribute to each other's growth and success. Such relationships create a sense of reciprocity, strengthening the bond over time.

5. Let Go of Relationships That No Longer Serve You

As challenging as it might be, parting ways with relationships that hinder your progress is crucial for personal and professional growth. Whether it's an unsupportive friendship, a toxic work environment, or even family members who drain your energy, prioritizing your well-being is essential.

Relationships that uplift versus those that hinder.

Relationships shape our emotional, mental, and even physical well-being. Some relationships uplift us, providing a foundation of support and encouragement, while others hinder our growth, draining energy and impeding progress. Understanding these dynamics' differences is essential for cultivating a fulfilling and purposeful life.

Characteristics of Uplifting Relationships

Uplifting relationships inspire and empower you to be your best self. They provide a sense of security, Positivity, and growth. Key traits include:

Emotional Support: These relationships offer a safe space to express yourself without fear of judgment. Whether facing challenges or celebrating successes, uplifting individuals provides empathy and understanding.

Encouragement and Motivation: People in uplifting relationships believe in their potential. They encourage you to pursue your goals, step out of your comfort zone, and strive for excellence.

Honest Feedback: Constructive criticism from trusted individuals helps you grow. Uplifting relationships provide honest and supportive feedback, fostering personal and professional development.

Positive Energy: Uplifting individuals radiate Positivity, which is contagious. Their optimism and outlook can inspire resilience and a proactive mindset.

Mutual Respect and Trust: These relationships are built on trust and mutual respect. Both parties value each other's boundaries, opinions, and contributions.

Signs Of Relationships That Hinder

Conversely, relationships that hinder you can negatively affect your mental and emotional health. These relationships often involve toxic behaviors or a lack of support, including:

Negativity and Criticism: Constant negativity or criticism can erode your confidence and self-worth. Such relationships often leave you feeling drained and unmotivated.

Lack of Support: Relationships that hinder fail to provide encouragement or understanding. These individuals may dismiss your aspirations or belittle your achievements.

Manipulation and Control: Toxic relationships often involve manipulation, where one party seeks to control or exploit the other. This behavior stifles personal growth and autonomy.

Jealousy and Competition: Instead of celebrating your successes, these individuals may feel threatened or envious, leading to an unhealthy rivalry dynamic.

Energy Drain: Hindered relationships are emotionally exhausting. They demand more from you than they give, leaving you feeling depleted rather than rejuvenated.

Navigating These Dynamics

To cultivate relationships that uplift while minimizing those that hinder, consider these steps:

Identify Positive Influences: Surround yourself with people who align with your values and contribute positively to your well-being. Look for traits such as integrity, optimism, and a growth-oriented mindset.

Set Boundaries: Establish clear boundaries in relationships that feel draining or toxic. Communicate your needs and protect your energy by limiting interactions when necessary.

Let Go When Needed: It can be difficult, but distancing yourself from relationships that consistently hinder your growth is essential. Prioritize your well-being and create space for healthier connections.

Invest in Uplifting Relationships: Nurture connections with those who inspire and support you. Make time for meaningful interactions and be an uplifting presence in their lives.

By consciously choosing relationships that uplift and addressing those that hinder, you can create a network of support and Positivity that aligns with your goals and aspirations.

The Gift of Mentorship

Mentorship is akin to offering a smile to the world—a simple yet profound gesture capable of leaving a lasting positive impact on someone's life. It is a gift that every individual has the power to give, a transformative opportunity to influence another's journey and guide them toward success. To mentor is to share the invaluable ability to support and guide, an act of generosity that extends its benefits beyond the mentee, enriching the mentor, the profession, and society. Much like a cherished tradition, the gift of mentorship is passed from generation to generation, fostering growth, wisdom, and shared purpose. Embracing the role of a mentor initiates a journey of self-discovery and immense fulfillment, where both the giver and receiver of mentorship are profoundly enriched.

While mentorship is not the same as parenting, it shares certain elements of guidance and nurturing. A mentor demonstrates patience and leadership, using their personal experiences not to dictate outcomes but to inspire and shape individualized guidance. Their role is not to impose a fixed trajectory on their mentees but to provide a starting point for open, dynamic dialogue. There is no rigid formula for mentorship—it is the connection between two minds, where the mentor illuminates a path, and the mentee embarks on an exciting journey to explore and embrace it.

The gift of mentorship comes with responsibilities, forming an implicit agreement between mentor and mentee to engage in a relationship grounded in trust and mutual respect. A mentor is a facilitator and teacher, empowering the mentee to captain their ship, navigate challenges, and learn from their experiences. Mentorship is not about eliminating obstacles but equipping the mentee with the skills to identify and overcome them. It is an enduring teaching relationship built on the mentor's belief in the mentee's potential and the mentee's trust in the mentor's guidance.

Relating this to The Gift of Mentorship, the process is an extraordinary exchange that offers fulfillment through the mentee's success. This "gift" embodies selflessness, patience, and the power to inspire change. It highlights the profound impact a mentor can have by helping mentees realize their potential, fostering a ripple effect that influences future generations. To mentor is to give freely of one's wisdom and experience, initiating a shared journey where the ultimate reward is the mentee's growth and achievements.

The Bible provides numerous examples of mentorship, with Elijah and Elisha standing out as a profound illustration of a mentor–mentee relationship. Their story, found in the books of 1 Kings and 2 Kings, highlights the transformative power of mentorship, showing how guidance and support can prepare someone to carry forward a divine mission.

Elijah and Elisha: The Mentor and the Successor

Elijah, a great prophet of Israel, became a mentor to Elisha when God directed him to anoint Elisha as his prophetic successor (1 Kings 19:16). From the moment Elisha left his home and livelihood to follow Elijah (1 Kings 19:19-21), their relationship demonstrated the key elements of mentorship:

Call to Mentorship: Elijah's invitation to Elisha to follow him represents the mentor's role in recognizing and nurturing potential. Elijah saw the calling on Elisha's life and acted as the catalyst for his prophetic journey.

Guidance and Training: Throughout their time together, Elijah provided spiritual training and insight, preparing Elisha for the challenges of prophetic ministry. This reflects the mentor's role as a teacher, sharing knowledge and experience to equip the mentee.

Modeling Leadership: Elijah's relationship with God and his acts of faith, such as calling fire from heaven (1 Kings 18:38), served as a powerful example for Elisha. A mentor's life often serves as a model for their mentee to emulate.

Encouragement to Seek Greater Things: Before Elijah was taken up to heaven in a whirlwind, Elisha requested a "double portion" of Elijah's Spirit (2 Kings 2:9). Elijah encouraged this bold request, reflecting a mentor's role in challenging their mentee to strive for greater accomplishments.

Passing the Mantle: Elijah's physical act of passing his cloak (mantle) to Elisha symbolized the transfer of authority and responsibility (2 Kings 2:13-15). This highlights the culmination of mentorship: equipping the mentee to continue the mentor's work independently.

Elisha's ministry following Elijah's departure exemplified the success of this mentorship. Elisha performed even greater miracles, fulfilling his request for a double portion of Elijah's Spirit (2 Kings 2:14-25, 2 Kings 4:1-44).

Other Biblical Examples of Mentorship

Moses and Joshua: Moses mentored Joshua, preparing him to lead Israel into the Promised Land. Moses taught Joshua leadership, faith, and reliance on God, empowering him to take on the mantle after Moses' death (Deuteronomy 34:9, Joshua 1:1-9).

Naomi and Ruth: Naomi served as a mentor to Ruth, guiding her in faith and practical matters after the loss of their husbands. Naomi's wisdom and advice ultimately led Ruth to a new life and her pivotal role in God's plan (Ruth 3:1-5).

Paul and Timothy: In the New Testament, Paul mentored Timothy, a young pastor, in faith, leadership, and ministry. Paul's letters to Timothy (1 and 2 Timothy) reflect the depth of this relationship, emphasizing encouragement, correction, and instruction (2 Timothy 1:6-7, 2 Timothy 3:10-17).

Jesus and His Disciples: Jesus exemplifies the ultimate mentor, guiding His disciples in faith, Character, and ministry. Over three years, He taught them through parables, miracles, and personal interactions, preparing them to continue His work after His ascension (Matthew 28:18-20, John 13:13-17).

Key Lessons from Biblical Mentorship

Mentorship involves recognizing potential and nurturing it.

A mentor provides guidance, encouragement, and opportunities for growth.

The relationship is built on trust, commitment, and mutual respect.

Mentorship aims to equip the mentee to carry on independently, often surpassing the mentor's achievements.

Encouraging Others on Their Journey

Passion fuels personal growth and success. It is a powerful motivator that unlocks potential and drives progress. Encouraging others to pursue their passions creates a ripple effect of Positivity and empowerment. This article will explore practical strategies for inspiring and supporting individuals on their journey toward achieving their dreams.

1. Understand and Value Their Interests

Begin by actively listening to their aspirations and interests. Engage them in conversations about their hobbies, goals, and dreams, showing genuine enthusiasm for their pursuits. This fosters a deeper connection and helps you identify what ignites their passion.

2. Reinforce Positivity

Small gestures of encouragement can have a lasting impact. Acknowledge their milestones, no matter how minor they may seem, and offer authentic praise. This positive reinforcement bolsters confidence and motivates them to persevere.

3. Inspire Through Your Example

Your actions and experiences can serve as a powerful source of inspiration. Share your journey, highlighting your challenges and the rewards of pursuing your passions. By witnessing your dedication, they may feel empowered to follow their path.

4. Foster a Nurturing Environment

Create a safe and supportive space where they feel encouraged to express their ideas and ambitions. Constructive feedback and accessible resources can help them refine their vision while ensuring they know they have a reliable source of guidance in you.

5. Guide Goal Setting

Help them translate their dreams into actionable goals. Break down overwhelming ambitions into manageable steps, making the process more achievable and less daunting. Clear, realistic objectives pave the way for consistent progress.

6. Motivate Through Encouragement

Everyone faces moments of doubt or distraction. Be a steady source of motivation, gently nudging them back on track and reminding them of their capabilities. An optimistic outlook can help them overcome challenges.

7. Provide Resources and Connections

Share valuable tools, networks, or opportunities if you have generous access to them. A well-timed connection or resource can often be the key to unlocking new possibilities.

8. Encourage Reflection and Mindfulness

Guide them toward self-reflection to clarify their passions and priorities. Understanding what truly brings them joy and fulfillment allows them to pursue their goals with greater focus and enthusiasm.

9. Celebrate Their Uniqueness

Remind them that their individuality is a strength. Their unique perspectives and talents differentiate them and add value to their journey. Encourage them to embrace their differences and use them to their advantage.

10. Exhibit Patience and Empathy

Recognize that growth takes time. Avoid rushing or pressuring them, allowing them to discover their path at their own pace. Your patience demonstrates your unwavering support.

11. Promote Healthy Risk-Taking

Encourage calculated risks that help them step out of their comfort zone. Reassure them that failures are opportunities for learning and growth. With each risk, they gain experience and resilience.

12. Balance Passion and Practicality

Help them integrate their passions with practical responsibilities. Striking a balance ensures they can pursue their dreams without compromising other important aspects of their life.

13. Be a Mentor, not a Dictator

Guide them with insight and wisdom, but allow them the freedom to make decisions. Empowering them to take ownership of their journey fosters independence and commitment.

14. Maintain Continuous Support

Support doesn't end with initial encouragement. Regularly follow up on their progress and be a consistent source of motivation. This ongoing investment in their growth can make a significant difference.

15. Believe in Their Potential

Sometimes, belief from another person can be transformative. Express your confidence in their abilities, inspiring them to believe in themselves.

16. Celebrate Effort and Progress

Acknowledging their attempts, successes, and failures reinforces the idea that every step is valuable. This approach helps them view setbacks as stepping stones rather than obstacles.

17. Highlight Their Progress

When discouragement arises, remind them of their achievements and growth. Celebrating how far they've come can reignite their passion and determination.

18. Advocate Lifelong Learning

Encourage them to view their passion as a lifelong journey. Continuous learning and skill-building will deepen their expertise and keep their enthusiasm alive.

19. Encourage Organization

Help them develop strategies to stay organized and focused. Effective time management and goal-setting tools can enhance their productivity and sense of control.

20. Promote Collaboration

Passion thrives in Collaboration. Encourage them to connect with like-minded individuals, exchange ideas, and explore opportunities for joint efforts.

21. Emphasize the Joy of the Journey

Remind them that fulfillment lies in the destination and the process itself. Savoring small victories and appreciating the journey enriches their experience and fosters a positive outlook.

By actively supporting others in pursuing their passions, you contribute to a culture of growth and achievement. When individuals feel empowered to follow their dreams, they inspire others, creating a ripple effect of motivation and fulfillment that uplifts everyone around them.

The mutual benefit of encouragement and accountability.

Encouragement and accountability are powerful forces that benefit the individual being supported and foster growth and development for those providing the support. This dynamic creates a symbiotic relationship where both parties thrive, learning from and inspiring one another.

Encouragement as a Catalyst for Growth

Encouragement fuels confidence and motivation, helping individuals push through challenges and maintain focus on their goals. When people receive genuine support, they feel valued, boosting their resilience and willingness to take risks. Encouragement is also contagious—when you uplift someone, it often inspires you to reflect on your journey, fostering a cycle of Positivity and personal growth.

Accountability Strengthens Commitment

Accountability adds structure and discipline to this relationship. When you hold someone accountable, you encourage them to stay consistent and take actionable steps toward their objectives. At the same time, being responsible for supporting others enhances your sense of responsibility and deepens your investment in their success. This reciprocal accountability strengthens the bond between both parties and drives collective progress.

The Interplay of Encouragement and Accountability

Combining encouragement with accountability ensures that support is both uplifting and constructive. For example, when you motivate someone to pursue their passion, offering gentle reminders or checking in on their progress ensures they stay on track. This balance creates a supportive yet focused environment where growth feels achievable and sustainable.

In your practice, encouraging and holding others accountable—whether learners, colleagues, or peers—fosters mutual growth. You inspire them to achieve their full potential while reinforcing your persistence, empathy, and leadership values. Together, encouragement and accountability form a partnership that empowers everyone involved to reach new heights.

Healing and Forgiveness

Who among us hasn't been hurt by the words or actions of another? It might have been a parent whose criticism shaped your childhood, a colleague who undermined your efforts, or a partner who betrayed your trust. Perhaps your pain stems from a deeply traumatic experience, such as emotional or physical abuse by someone you held dear. These experiences often leave lingering scars of resentment, anger, and bitterness — emotions that can be overwhelming and enduring.

However, holding onto pain often hurts the bearer more than anyone else. Choosing forgiveness can pave the way for peace and hope, offering a profound journey toward physical, emotional, and spiritual well-being.

Understanding Forgiveness

Forgiveness holds unique meanings for different individuals. At its core, forgiveness involves deliberately releasing resentment and anger. While the pain of what transpired may never fully disappear, forgiveness diminishes its grip on your life. By letting go, you free yourself from the control of the one who caused you harm. Forgiveness can also foster empathy, compassion, and understanding toward the person who hurt you.

Importantly, forgiveness does not imply excusing or forgetting the harm inflicted upon you. Nor does it necessarily lead to reconciliation. Rather, forgiveness brings an inner peace that allows you to focus on yourself and move forward with your life.

Benefits of Forgiveness

The benefits of forgiveness extend across mental, emotional, and physical dimensions, profoundly impacting overall well-being. Embracing forgiveness promotes psychological health by alleviating stress, reducing negative emotions, and fostering more fulfilling and harmonious relationships.

Physical Health Benefits

Forgiveness contributes significantly to physical health, including:

Lower Blood Pressure: By reducing chronic stress and hostility, forgiveness supports a stable cardiovascular system, lowering the risk of hypertension.

Stronger Immune Function: Those who practice forgiveness often experience improved immunity, making them less ill-prone.

Relief from Chronic Pain: Releasing grudges can alleviate stress-related pain, contributing to overall physical comfort.

Improved Heart Health: Forgiveness reduces the physiological effects of chronic anger and resentment, such as elevated heart rate and blood pressure, decreasing the likelihood of heart disease.

Enhancing Relationships

Forgiveness plays a pivotal role in strengthening and repairing interpersonal connections:

Healing Fractured Relationships: By letting go of resentment, individuals can rebuild trust and nurture open communication.

Fostering Compassion: Forgiveness often deepens empathy and understanding, encouraging a more compassionate view of others' imperfections.

Reducing Emotional Baggage: Forgiving frees individuals from the emotional weight of past hurts, paving the way for healthier, more genuine interactions.

Personal Empowerment through Forgiveness

Forgiveness is a powerful act of self-empowerment that enables individuals to reclaim their emotional and mental autonomy:

Reclaiming Control: Letting go of anger and pain restores personal power, preventing these emotions from dominating one's life.

Boosting Self-Esteem: Forgiving and addressing one's imperfections fosters self-acceptance and personal growth.

Cultivating Positivity: Releasing grudges allows individuals to embrace hope and optimism, promoting a forward-looking perspective.

Embracing forgiveness can yield transformative benefits, such as:

- Building healthier and more fulfilling relationships.
- Enhancing mental health by reducing symptoms of depression, anxiety, and stress.
- Lowering blood pressure and promoting heart health.
- Strengthening the immune system.
- Cultivating improved self-esteem and a positive outlook on life.

The Struggle to Forgive

Forgiveness is often easier said than done, especially when betrayal or harm is inflicted by someone you deeply care for. Dwelling on painful events can nurture grudges filled with bitterness and resentment. Over time, these negative emotions can overshadow positive ones, leading to a sense of injustice or emotional turmoil.

While some individuals naturally find forgiveness easier, everyone can cultivate this ability.

Consequences of Holding Grudges

Failing to forgive can have far-reaching effects, such as:

- Carrying anger and bitterness into new relationships and experiences.
- Feeling trapped in the past and unable to enjoy the present.
- Experiencing heightened anxiety, irritability, or depression.
- Facing inner conflict with your spiritual beliefs.
- Losing meaningful connections with others.

Moving Toward Forgiveness

Forgiveness requires intention and practice. Here are steps to help you embrace it:

Acknowledge the Value of Forgiveness: Recognize how forgiving others can transform your life.

Identify What Needs Healing: Reflect on the source of your pain and who you need to forgive.

Seek Support: Join a support group or consult a counselor to guide your healing journey.

Process Your Emotions: Understand how the harm has shaped your behavior and work toward releasing those feelings.

Choose to Forgive: Make the conscious decision to let go of resentment.

Reclaim Your Power: Free yourself from the control the offending person or situation has over you.

Navigating Challenges in Forgiveness

Forgiving someone who refuses to acknowledge their wrongdoing can be particularly difficult. In such cases:

- Practice empathy by trying to view the situation from their perspective.
- Reflect on possible circumstances that influenced their actions.
- Consider moments when others have forgiven you.
- Utilize tools like journaling, meditation, or spiritual practices to process your emotions.
- Forgiveness is a journey, not a one-time act. Even minor hurts may need revisiting as part of your growth.

Forgiveness and Reconciliation

While forgiveness can sometimes lead to reconciliation, it is not guaranteed or required. Reconciliation depends on the willingness and circumstances of both parties. Even if reconciliation isn't possible or appropriate, forgiveness can still provide inner peace and closure.

The Role of Forgiveness in Healing

Healing through forgiveness is a deeply personal journey. It doesn't mean condoning harmful behavior but freeing yourself from its emotional hold. Forgiveness restores your focus on personal growth, emotional balance, and spiritual fulfillment, fostering a renewed sense of agency over your life.

Seeking Forgiveness

If you are the one seeking forgiveness, start by reflecting on the harm you've caused and its impact on others. Express genuine remorse without justifying your actions and extend an earnest request for forgiveness. Forgiveness is a process for both parties, and healing may take time. Commit to treating others with compassion and empathy as you move forward.

Ultimately, forgiveness is an act of self-liberation. By choosing to forgive, you grant yourself the gift of healing, allowing room for peace, resilience, and growth to flourish.

How Unresolved Hurt Impacts Presence.

Unresolved hurt can significantly impact one's ability to be fully present in personal and professional situations. When emotional wounds remain unaddressed, they can affect mental, emotional, and even physical well-being, often manifesting in various ways that hinder one's ability to engage fully with the present moment.

Emotional Drainage and Mental Distraction

Unresolved hurt tends to keep the mind preoccupied with past events, fostering a cycle of rumination. This mental distraction prevents individuals from being fully immersed in their current experiences, whether in conversations, work tasks, or personal activities. Instead of focusing on the here and now, the mind may constantly replay the hurtful event or imagine potential conflicts. This emotional baggage can create a state of constant inner turmoil, leading to difficulty maintaining attention or being emotionally available to others.

Emotional Reactivity and Impaired Relationships

When hurt is unresolved, individuals often carry emotional scars that can trigger disproportionate reactions in everyday situations. Small disagreements or misunderstandings may evoke intense emotional responses, clouding judgment and preventing clear communication. This emotional reactivity impacts relationships, making engaging in constructive dialogues or fully empathizing with others harder. As a result, personal and professional connections can become strained, and meaningful interactions can be overshadowed by past pain.

Physical Manifestations and Energy Drain

Unresolved hurt also impacts one's physical state, as emotional distress often manifests physically through tension, fatigue, or even chronic pain. The constant weight of unresolved emotions can drain energy, leaving individuals feeling mentally and physically exhausted. This energy depletion further detracts from one's ability to be present at the moment, as much of their focus is diverted toward managing emotional or physical discomfort.

Impaired Self-Awareness and Growth

When hurt is not processed and healed, individuals may find it challenging to be aware of their emotions in real-time. This lack of self-awareness makes it difficult to recognize how unresolved pain might be influencing thoughts, actions, and reactions. Personal growth can be stunted without actively addressing these wounds, as emotional and psychological healing cannot occur. Over time, this emotional stagnation can prevent one from embracing new opportunities or evolving into a healthier version of themselves.

Impact on Mindfulness and Presence

Mindfulness requires individuals to be fully attuned to the present moment, yet unresolved hurt creates mental and emotional clutter. Mindfulness becomes increasingly difficult when the mind is bogged down by unresolved pain, preventing the individual from fully immersed in experiences like conversations, activities, or self-reflection. The past intrudes on the present, diminishing one's capacity for awareness, acceptance, and joy in what is happening.

In essence, unresolved hurt is a barrier to fully embracing life, draining emotional energy, distorting perceptions, and impairing relationships. To cultivate presence, it's crucial to confront and heal past wounds, as doing so not only clears the mind and heart but also empowers individuals to engage more deeply with the present, fostering richer connections and personal fulfillment.

Reflection Questions

How has community influenced your personal and spiritual growth? What steps can you take to build a stronger support network?

Are the relationships in your life uplifting or hindering your growth? How can you create boundaries with those who may hold you back?

Who has been a mentor in your life, and how have they shaped your journey? How can you emulate Elijah's guidance with others?

In what ways can you encourage and hold others accountable while pursuing healing and forgiveness in your own life?

Actions

Identify one community or group to actively engage with for personal and spiritual growth.

Reflect on your current circle of relationships and adjust as needed to align with your values and goals.

Seek out or become a mentor, modeling biblical examples like Elijah and Elisha.

Practice forgiveness by addressing unresolved hurt and offering encouragement to others, fostering mutual healing.

Chapter Five
Spiritual Alignment

Spiritual Alignment fosters a deep connection and harmony with your higher self, the Universe, or a higher power. It entails synchronizing your thoughts, beliefs, actions, and intentions with your spiritual values and overarching purpose.

When you achieve spiritual alignment, you experience inner peace, clarity, and a profound sense of purpose. This Alignment empowers you to live authentically and make decisions that reflect your highest good and spiritual truth.

How to Achieve Spiritual Alignment

The journey toward spiritual Alignment is a deeply personal experience that looks different for each individual. However, certain practices can support this process:

Self-reflection and introspection: Regularly assessing your thoughts, behaviors, and beliefs can help uncover and realign your true values.

Meditation and mindfulness: These practices calm the mind, allowing you to connect with your inner self and your spiritual core.

Connecting with nature: Nature's tranquility fosters a sense of peace and deepens your connection to the world around you.

Practicing gratitude: Focusing on what you are thankful for shifts your energy towards Positivity and abundance.

Engaging in spiritual practices or rituals: Rituals help ground you in your faith and maintain focus on your spiritual path.

Surround yourself with positive, like-minded individuals: Being around others who support your spiritual growth can elevate your energy and align you with your purpose.

Signs of Spiritual Alignment

When you are spiritually aligned, you may experience:

A profound sense of inner peace and contentment.

Heightened intuition and mental clarity.

An increased awareness of synchronicities, feeling that the Universe is guiding you.

Being in a flow state where things unfold effortlessly, and manifestations occur more readily.

A deep connection to something greater than yourself provides a sense of belonging and purpose.

How to Become Spiritually Aligned

Engaging in self-reflection, meditation, and connecting with nature is important for becoming spiritually aligned. Experiment with different spiritual practices to discover what resonates most with your journey. Trust that spiritual Alignment will unfold as you explore and nurture your inner wisdom.

What Does Alignment Mean in a Person?

In an individual, Alignment refers to harmony with their true self and life purpose. It involves living in a way that reflects their core values, beliefs, and intentions, creating a balanced and purposeful life.

What Does Spiritual Alignment Feel Like?

Spiritual Alignment feels like a profound sense of peace and contentment, accompanied by clarity, heightened intuition, and a deep understanding of the interconnectedness of all things. It provides a feeling of being "in tune" with the Universe and your place within it.

What Does it Mean to Seek Alignment?

Seeking Alignment involves actively seeking a state where your thoughts, actions, and intentions are in harmony with your higher self and spiritual values. It means exploring practices, beliefs, and rituals that align with your greater purpose and help you live authentically. This pursuit is an ongoing process that fosters spiritual growth and transformation.

By relating to spiritual Alignment, you can create a life that is true to your deepest self and connected to the larger, universal flow of energy. It's an ongoing practice of staying aligned with your higher purpose and living authentically.

Deepening Your Prayer Life

Prayer serves as the primary means of communication with God, encompassing various forms such as prayers of praise, sorrow, joy, and thanksgiving, as illustrated throughout the Bible. At its core, prayer is about fostering a deep and intimate relationship with the Lord. Just as conversations are essential to strengthening relationships with friends, prayer plays a critical role in deepening one's relationship with God. Without it, spiritual growth is limited. One must actively nurture one's prayer life to draw closer to God.

In addition to being a form of communication, prayer is an act of worship. We express our awe and reverence for God's greatness and deeds through prayer. The focus of prayer should always be on God rather than on ourselves. Jesus exemplified the perfect model of prayer in Matthew 6:9-13, and His prayers offer valuable insights into how we should communicate with God.

Modeling Our Prayer Life After Jesus

In the Gospels, Jesus demonstrates how and whom to pray for and what attitude to adopt. By following His example, we can cultivate a deeper connection with God.

In John 17:20, Jesus prayed for His disciples and those who would come to faith through their testimony.

"I do not pray for these alone, but also for those who will believe in Me through their word…" — John 17:20.

In Matthew 26:39, Jesus demonstrated submission to God's will, even in intense suffering.

"He went a little farther and fell on His face, and prayed, saying, 'O My Father, if it is possible, let this cup pass from Me; nevertheless, not as I will, but as You will.'" — Matthew 26:39.

Jesus also modeled the importance of spending time alone in prayer.

"Now it came to pass in those days that He went out to the mountain to pray, and continued all night in prayer to God." — Luke 6:12.

Furthermore, He withdrew from crowds to find quiet places for communion with His Father.

"And when He had sent the multitudes away, He went up on the mountain to pray. Now when evening came, He was alone there." — Matthew 14:23.

7 Ways to Deepen Your Prayer Life

By emulating Jesus' prayer life, we can draw closer to God. Here are seven practical steps to enhance your prayer life and nurture an intimate relationship with God.

Make Prayer Your Priority

"Rejoice always, pray without ceasing, and in everything, give thanks; for this is the will of God in Christ Jesus for you." — 1 Thessalonians 5:16-18

Praying without ceasing can seem overwhelming, but God encourages a prayerful attitude throughout daily life. Set aside a dedicated space for quiet time each day, and use reminders like sticky notes or prayer requests around your home to help keep prayer a priority.

Use Prayer as an Opportunity to Learn More About God

"The fear of the Lord is the beginning of wisdom, and the knowledge of the Holy One is understanding." — Proverbs 9:10

Prayer is a way to learn more about God's Character and develop reverence for Him. Ask God to reveal more of His nature to you, and as you grow in understanding, you will gain wisdom and respect for His holiness.

Pray for God to Align Your Will with His

"Teach me to do Your will, for You are my God; Your Spirit is good. Lead me in the land of uprightness." — Psalm 143:10

Jesus focused on fulfilling God's will throughout His ministry. Our prayer should align our desires with God's plan, even if it requires personal sacrifice or difficult obedience. God provides the strength needed to follow His will.

Reflect on God's Faithfulness When Praying

"Through the Lord's mercies, we are not consumed because His compassions fail not. They are new every morning; great is Your faithfulness." — Lamentations 3:22-23

Remember God's faithfulness in your prayers. Praise Him for His mercy, guidance, and provision. Keeping a prayer journal to track answered prayers can be a powerful reminder of His faithfulness.

Don't Feel You Must Have All the Right Words

"Likewise, the Spirit also helps with our weaknesses. For we do not know what we should pray for as we ought, but the Spirit Himself makes intercession for us with groanings which cannot be uttered." — Romans 8:26

You don't need perfect words to approach God in prayer. God understands your needs even when you cannot find the words. Being honest and transparent in your prayers will help you connect more deeply with Him.

Listen to How God Responds to Your Prayers

"My sheep hear My voice, and I know them, and they follow Me." — John 10:27

Prayer is not just a one-way conversation. God communicates through His Word, the Holy Spirit, and wise counsel. Be open and attentive to His responses, and be ready to act obediently.

Pray with Others

"As iron sharpens iron, so a man sharpens the countenance of his friend." — Proverbs 27:17

Praying with others brings accountability and encouragement. Sharing prayer requests with fellow believers can strengthen your faith, deepen your commitment to prayer, and offer support through life's challenges.

These seven steps can help you create a more intimate prayer life, deepen your relationship with God, and experience His presence in new and profound ways.

Techniques for meaningful and consistent prayer.

Developing a consistent prayer life is essential for any believer who seeks a deeper, more intimate connection with God. However, establishing a steadfast prayer routine can be challenging amidst the busyness of life. Prayer offers a unique opportunity to connect with our loving heavenly Father, who provides us with His guidance, presence, and purpose through heartfelt conversations.

However, maintaining a dynamic prayer life demands both commitment and intentionality. Distractions often encroach upon our scheduled prayer time, and good intentions can quickly fade into sporadic prayers. To overcome this, we need practical guidance to help us pray consistently. The following ten steps offer simple yet powerful ways to develop a consistent prayer life. Incorporating even a few of these practices into your daily routine will enrich your spiritual journey.

With focused effort, prayer will become a cornerstone of your spiritual walk, allowing you to experience the joy of conversing with God daily.

1. Set Aside a Specific Time for Daily Prayer

The first step to developing a consistent prayer life is setting aside a specific time each day to connect with God. Treat your prayer time as a daily appointment, as non-negotiable as breakfast or your morning commute. Choose a time that fits realistically into your daily schedule, one you can maintain even amidst life's demands.

Many believers find that praying first thing in the morning sets a positive tone for the day. The quiet of early morning provides a peaceful atmosphere to connect with God. Waking up 15 to 30 minutes earlier can provide space for meaningful prayer before your mind is consumed with the day's tasks. Others prefer midday or evening prayers, such as during lunch breaks or before bed.

Whatever time you choose, be realistic about the duration. Start with small steps—5 to 10 minutes—then gradually increase the time as your schedule allows. Consistency, not length, is the key. Like any relationship, your closeness with God will grow through regular communication.

For more accountability, be specific in scheduling your prayer time. Instead of a vague "morning prayer," mark a precise time—e.g., "6:35-7:05 am"—in your calendar. Treat this appointment with God as you would an important meeting, protecting this time from other distractions.

Although developing this habit requires commitment, it will bring immeasurable rewards as you start your day grounded in God's presence.

2. Designate a Special Place to Pray

In addition to a consistent time, having a designated prayer space can help enhance your focus and connection with God. Choose a quiet, distraction-free location where you can meet God regularly—whether in your home, office, or another private area.

Consider making this space visually and sensorially inspiring. Use elements like candles, worship music, or Scripture verses to create an atmosphere of reverence. Engaging your senses through prayer beads, kneeling, or other postures can further deepen your connection.

This space should become a sacred place where you meet with God. Over time, your mind and heart will associate this spot with meaningful, uninterrupted time in His presence. Let this space remind you to leave behind distractions and enter deep communion with God.

3. Pray with Purpose

Approaching prayer with purpose helps avoid aimless wandering. Come to your prayer time each day with a clear direction—to praise God, confess, give thanks, or intercede for others. A helpful framework for prayer is the ACTS model: Adoration, Confession, Thanksgiving, and Supplication.

Start by adoring God for His attributes, then confess any sins and ask for forgiveness. Follow by giving thanks for the blessings in your life, and finish with supplication—interceding for the needs of others. You can also use the Lord's Prayer as a model to guide your prayers, focusing on each part related to your current circumstances.

Praying through Scripture is another powerful way to deepen your prayer life. Meditate on a specific verse or passage and let it guide your conversation with God. Engaging your heart and mind while remaining sensitive to the Holy Spirit's leading will make your prayer time more meaningful.

4. Vary Your Prayer Methods

Our relationship with God thrives through creativity and variety in our communication. Try different prayer methods, postures, and tools to keep your daily prayer time fresh and engaging. You can explore singing, journaling, using prayer beads, or praying through the Tabernacle.

Switching up your body posture—kneeling, standing, or walking—can help you stay focused. Don't hesitate to experiment with creative ways to express your prayers, such as through art, music, or poetry. Fasting and serving others are also powerful ways to draw nearer to God.

Varying the length of your prayer sessions can also provide a fresh perspective. Try occasional extended prayer times, such as retreats or vigils, for a deeper connection with God.

5. Set Prayer Goals and Track Progress

Setting tangible prayer goals can provide motivation and a sense of accomplishment. Start by setting achievable frequency and time goals. Track your progress in a prayer journal to help you stay consistent and review your journey.

Set incremental and content-based goals, such as focusing on different types of prayer (adoration, confession, intercession) or praying through specific Scripture passages. Review your goals regularly to track your growth and make adjustments as needed.

Remember, prayer is a journey—not a competition. Celebrate your progress and remain flexible as you grow in your communication with God.

Incorporating these steps into your daily life will help establish a consistent, vibrant prayer routine. Through commitment and creativity, your relationship with God will deepen, and your prayer life will become a natural, enriching part of your spiritual walk.

Listening to God's Voice

When life feels overwhelming, and we are consumed by worry or anxiety, we often turn to God, longing for His voice to guide us. These moments of need frequently drive us to seek His direction. The comforting truth is that God is always ready to listen and speak to us, desiring a connection with each of us.

God continuously reaches out to His people, yet many miss His voice because they only seek Him during crises or major decisions. Confusion and frustration often follow when they fail to discern His guidance. Questions arise: How do I hear from God? Why isn't He speaking to me? However, it doesn't have to be this way. God wants you to listen to Him clearly during difficult times and as part of an ongoing relationship.

Rather than relying on formulas or quick fixes, the key to hearing God is cultivating a deep and consistent relationship with Him. The closer you grow to God, the more naturally you will recognize His voice in everyday moments. These conversations will transform you into who He created you to be, shaping your life according to His plans.

Here are ten ways to help you hear God's voice consistently and recognize His guidance:

1. Understand You Were Created for a Close Relationship with God

God designed you for a deep friendship with Him. In this connection, you'll hear Him best. His will is for you to engage in regular conversations with Him, enabling you to understand His Character and become more like Jesus. Through these interactions, you'll experience His presence and wisdom moment by moment.

Download Our Free Guide, Discerning the Voice of God in Your Life – A 30-Day Prayer Guide, to help you listen to God regularly.

2. Examine Your Motives for Seeking God

Reflect on why you want to hear from God. Are you genuinely open to His guidance, ready to follow even when challenging? Or is your desire driven by selfish motives, such as seeking comfort or validation? Confess any wrong intentions and ask God to align your heart with His purposes.

3. Prioritize a Relationship Over a Message

Hearing from God is essential, but your ultimate goal should be developing spiritual maturity and a close relationship with Him. As you grow in intimacy with God, His voice will become clearer, and His guidance will naturally align with your walk with Him.

4. Approach God with Confidence and Humility

Know that you matter deeply to God. He is willing to speak to you as powerfully as He did to the people in the Bible. At the same time, remain humble, recognizing that receiving His guidance requires an attitude of surrender and faith.

5. Wait Patiently for God's Timing

You cannot force God to speak on demand. Instead, focus on building a respectful, trusting relationship and wait for Him to communicate when the time is right. If God remains silent, consider whether your decision aligns with biblical principles and move forward in faith, knowing His will encompasses freedom within those boundaries.

6. Recognize the Many Ways God Speaks

God communicates in various ways: through Scripture, prayer, circumstances, and the counsel of others. While dramatic experiences like visions or miraculous signs may occur, God often speaks gently and quietly, prompting your thoughts and heart. The closer your relationship with Him, the more attentive you'll be to His still, small voice.

7. Renew Your Mind Daily

God speaks through your mind, but to hear Him clearly, it must be renewed. Romans 12:2 urges: "Do not conform to the pattern of this world but be transformed by the renewing of your mind." Invite the Holy Spirit to cleanse your thoughts of negativity, false beliefs, and distractions. Let Him replace them with truth and wisdom that align with God's will.

8. Engage with the Living Word

The Bible is God's written Word but becomes alive through Jesus, the Living Word. When you read Scripture prayerfully, invite Jesus to make the words resonate deeply, infusing your heart with His faith and love. Let the Bible's truths shape and transform your life.

9. Learn to Recognize God's Voice

Over time, you can discern God's voice through experience. His messages will never contradict Scripture and often carry a sense of peace, authority, and reasonableness. If you sense God is speaking, seek confirmation through prayer, Scripture, circumstances, or the impressions of the Holy Spirit.

10. Create Space to Listen

Set aside time each day to listen intentionally for God's voice. This practice will strengthen your ability to hear Him and deepen your relationship. Journaling your experiences can help you reflect on His messages and track how He works in your life.

God desires for you to recognize His voice and walk closely with Him. As you develop the habit of listening, you will discover His promises and plans for you unfolding. Begin today, trusting that God is already speaking – and that He wants you to hear

The Role of Worship

Worship is an integral aspect of the Christian faith, acting as a profound expression of love, reverence, and devotion to God. It transcends routine rituals, offering a transformative and intimate connection between believers and the divine. Worship is a sacred dialogue, fostering a deep sense of communion with God and aligning the human Spirit with His presence. In exploring the role of worship, we uncover its biblical foundations, ability to nurture personal and spiritual growth, and significance in shaping a lifestyle of devotion. Furthermore, we examine the role of music, the communal dimension of worship, and its extension beyond church walls into everyday life, illustrating this practice's profound and holistic impact.

Worship, at its core, aligns with God's will. It transcends the boundaries of mere rituals and traditions, becoming a profound expression of surrender and obedience to God. When believers worship, they consciously attune their hearts, minds, and spirits to the divine purpose and calling for their lives. This Alignment reflects a commitment to acknowledging God's sovereignty, embracing His guidance, and living by His principles.

Through worship, believers are reminded of their identity in Christ and their role within the broader framework of God's kingdom. Acts of worship—whether through prayer, song, or acts of service—become opportunities to reaffirm faith and seek God's direction. In the quiet moments of devotion or the communal gatherings of praise, worship transforms into a dynamic interaction where believers listen for God's voice and respond with faith-driven action.

The Bible underscores this concept of Alignment in passages such as Romans 12:1-2, where Paul urges believers to offer their bodies as living sacrifices, holy and pleasing to God, as an act of spiritual worship. This call to worship involves a transformation of mind and a rejection of worldly patterns, fostering a deeper understanding of God's will.

Worship as Alignment also extends to everyday life. It inspires believers to reflect God's Character in their decisions, relationships, and interactions. By aligning their lives with God's will, they become living testaments to His love and grace, allowing worship to permeate every aspect of their existence. This holistic view of worship deepens personal faith and serves as a witness to others, drawing them toward the transformative power of God's presence.

Understanding Worship in the Christian Journey

The Essence and Significance of Worship

Worship in Christianity is far more than a scheduled gathering for song and sermon. It is a dynamic encounter with the divine, allowing believers to express their gratitude, devotion, and awe. Rooted in acknowledging God's sovereignty, worship becomes a spiritual anchor, refocusing the heart on what truly matters. It strengthens faith, fosters a sense of purpose, and enables believers to live their daily lives as an act of reverence to God.

Worship as Connection: Experiencing God Through Song and Praise

Encountering God's Presence in Worship

Worship creates sacred moments of connection, transporting believers into God's presence. Through heartfelt praise, individuals experience peace, joy, and renewal. This holy practice bridges the physical and spiritual realms, offering direct communication with the Creator.

The Emotional and Spiritual Impact of Worship

Worship is more than intellectual engagement; it stirs profound emotions, offering healing for brokenness, solace during trials, and a renewed sense of hope. It uplifts and rejuvenates the soul, empowering believers to face challenges with resilience grounded in God's promises.

Worship's Biblical Foundations: Grounding in Scripture

Old Testament Principles and Practices

The Old Testament offers a wealth of examples, from David's Psalms to the sacrificial rituals in the Tabernacle, illustrating worship as an expression of gratitude, repentance, and surrender. These practices emphasize the heart's posture over external actions, a relevant principle today.

New Testament Teachings on Worship

Jesus redefined worship as a spiritual practice rooted in "spirit and truth" (John 4:24). Early Christians exemplified this through communal worship, prayers, and shared fellowship, demonstrating that worship transcends location and becomes a lifestyle aligned with God's love and purpose.

Worship as a Lifestyle: Living Praise Beyond Church Walls

Incorporating Worship into Daily Life

Worship is not confined to Sunday mornings. It can be integrated into personal devotions, prayerful reflection, and acts of kindness. Whether in quiet moments of gratitude or through mindful work and relationships, worship transforms ordinary life into an offering to God.

Living Worship Through Actions

True worship is reflected in daily choices, embodying love, humility, and grace. By honoring God in our work, relationships, and decisions, we live as a testament to His goodness, extending worship beyond liturgy into every sphere of life.

The Transformative Power of Worship

Deepening Faith and Spiritual Growth

Worship is a conduit for deepening one's relationship with God. Through it, believers invite God's transformative presence, aligning their hearts with His will and growing in spiritual maturity.

Healing and Restoration Through Worship

In moments of brokenness, worship becomes a sanctuary for healing and renewal. It provides comfort and assurance and reminds us of God's unwavering care and sovereignty over life's circumstances.

The Role of Music: Enhancing the Worship Experience

Music as a Vehicle for Worship

Music holds a unique power to connect the heart to God. Its melodies and lyrics transcend spoken words, inspiring deeper reflection and devotion. Whether through a jubilant hymn or a quiet chorus, music fosters an atmosphere of worship that resonates with the soul.

Curating Worship Music

Carefully chosen songs amplify worship's impact, ensuring the message aligns with the congregation's spiritual needs. Thoughtful selection enhances collective praise and creates meaningful encounters with God.

Corporate Worship: Unity in the Body of Christ

The Significance of Gathering Together

Corporate worship unites believers, fostering a sense of belonging and shared purpose. It allows for mutual encouragement and collective glorification of God, strengthening individual and communal faith.

The Richness of Community Worship

Diverse expressions of worship within a community create a tapestry of praise reflecting God's kingdom's universal nature. Through shared experiences, believers grow in understanding and appreciation of worship's multifaceted beauty.

Worship Beyond the Church: A Witness to God's Glory

Extending Worship into Everyday Life

Worship transcends Sunday services, becoming a lifestyle of devotion and gratitude. As believers align their actions with God's will, their lives testify to His love, drawing others to encounter Him.

Cultivating a Worshipful Life

Living with intentionality, believers can glorify God in their daily interactions, workplaces, and communities, bringing the essence of worship into all aspects of life.

Finding Rest in God

Rest in the Lord is a recurring theme in the Bible, signifying far more than physical rest. When the psalmist exhorts, "Rest in the LORD, and wait patiently for Him" (Psalm 37:7, NKJV), it calls for a spiritual stillness—a release from anxiety, worry, and futile human efforts. This rest is a break from internal and external struggles, peace in God's presence, and surrender to His sovereign care.

The Hebrew term "rest" conveys peace, calm, and quietness before God. Different Bible translations capture this idea with phrases like "Be still before the Lord" (ESV, NIV), "Be silent before the Lord" (CSB), and "Surrender yourself to the Lord" (GW). Each highlights the importance of dwelling in God's presence and trusting His lordship as the pathway to true rest.

In the Old Testament, God promised His people a life of peace in the Promised Land, contingent on their faithfulness to Him (Exodus 33:14; Joshua 1:13–15). However, when Israel strayed from God, they forfeited this rest, as seen in Psalm 95:7–11. The captivity in Babylon and their eventual return revealed again the call to trust and rest in God. Through the prophet Jeremiah, God reassured Israel of His promise: "Israel will return to a life of peace, and no one will terrorize them" (Jeremiah 30:10, NLT). Yet, their failure to live righteously hindered them from fully experiencing this rest, as Isaiah declared: "The fruit of that righteousness will be peace; its effect will be quietness and confidence forever" (Isaiah 32:17).

The New Testament offers a deeper understanding of this rest through Jesus Christ. The book of Hebrews explains that believers in Christ enter God's rest by faith: "For only we who believe can enter his rest" (Hebrews 4:3, NLT). This rest is a present reality and a future promise, culminating in eternal earthly rest (Hebrews 4:9–11). In the here and now, Jesus invites us to bring our burdens to Him: "Come to me, all of you who are weary and carry heavy burdens, and I will give you rest" (Matthew 11:28–30, NLT). Through His gentle and humble nature, He provides rest for our souls, offering peace amid life's storms.

This peace does not eliminate life's difficulties but transforms how we respond to them. Rather than succumbing to worry or frantic attempts to resolve our challenges, we can rest in the Lord's presence, trusting Him to care for us. The Apostle Paul reminds believers to bring all their anxieties to God in prayer, coupled with thanksgiving, and in return, experience God's peace that guards their hearts and minds (Philippians 4:6–7).

Finding rest in God is deeply connected to this concept of resting in the Lord. It involves quieting our hearts, surrendering our plans and anxieties, and abiding in His presence. Isaiah's vision of God, "high and lifted" (Isaiah 6:1), reminds us of His sovereignty over everything, including every struggle we face. As we acknowledge His power and faithfully wait on Him, we experience the profound peace that only He can provide. This rest is a momentary reprieve and a sustaining strength, enabling us to face life with confidence and hope.

Finding rest in God is about living in trust and surrender, rooted in His promises and faithfulness. It is an ongoing act of dwelling in His presence, releasing our burdens to Him, and allowing His peace to reign in our hearts. This is the rest that the Lord offers—a rest that transforms our lives brings clarity to our souls and aligns us with His divine purpose.

Sabbath practices and rest are essential for renewal, both spiritually and physically. Rooted in the biblical tradition, the Sabbath is a divinely ordained rhythm of work and rest designed to restore the individual, the community, and the relationship between humanity and God. Observing the Sabbath emphasizes intentional withdrawal from daily labor to focus on spiritual rejuvenation, relational connections, and holistic well-being.

In the creation narrative, God established the pattern of Sabbath rest. After six days of creative work, God rested on the seventh day and blessed it as holy (Genesis 2:2–3). This divine example underscores the importance of stepping away from work to find renewal. The Sabbath is not merely about physical rest but about aligning oneself with God's design for life—living in a rhythm that honors productivity and restoration.

The Ten Commandments codified the Sabbath as a covenantal practice for the Israelites (Exodus 20:8–11). They were called to cease labor on the seventh day as a reminder of God's provision and an act of trust in His sovereignty. Beyond its theological significance, the Sabbath provided a practical opportunity for physical renewal, communal gathering, and spiritual reflection.

Jesus deepened the understanding of the Sabbath by emphasizing its purpose for humanity. He declared, "The Sabbath was made for man, not man for the Sabbath" (Mark 2:27, NIV). This statement highlights the Sabbath's restorative intent, prioritizing compassion, healing, and spiritual renewal over legalistic observance. By healing on the Sabbath, Jesus demonstrated that rest is not simply about inactivity but about engaging in life-giving practices that restore the soul and serve others.

Modern Sabbath practices reflect these principles and are vital for navigating the demands of contemporary life. In a culture often defined by busyness, intentionally setting aside time for rest helps individuals recover from stress, prevent burnout, and foster a sense of balance. Spiritual renewal is particularly significant, providing space for prayer, meditation, and reconnecting with God. Rest is also essential for cultivating relationships—with family and within one's community—strengthening bonds and fostering unity.

In addition to spiritual and relational benefits, Sabbath rest promotes mental and physical health. Studies show regular rest enhances cognitive function, emotional resilience, and overall well-being. It allows individuals to reset their focus, gain perspective, and approach challenges with renewed energy and creativity.

Sabbath practices, therefore, represent a holistic approach to renewal. By dedicating time to rest and spiritual connection, individuals honor God's design, find balance in their lives, and equip themselves to engage meaningfully in their work, relationships, and faith. Observing a Sabbath rhythm invites a deeper experience of renewal, empowering individuals to live with greater purpose and joy.

Staying immersed in God's Word fortifies the believer's Spirit, provides clarity amidst confusion, and ensures alignment with divine truths. Like a steady anchor in turbulent waters, the Scriptures keep us grounded, offering guidance, strength, and hope. By meditating on and applying these truths daily, we resist challenges and thrive in faith and purpose.

1 Peter 5:8

"Be sober-minded; be watchful. Your adversary, the devil, prowls around like a roaring lion, seeking someone to devour."

This verse emphasizes vigilance and spiritual awareness. Believers can guard against the enemy's subtle and persistent attacks by staying rooted in the Word.

Hebrews 4:12

"The word of God is living and active, sharper than any two-edged sword, piercing to the division of soul and spirit, of joints and marrow, and discerning the thoughts and intentions of the heart."

The Word is not passive; it is dynamic and transformative, cutting through falsehoods and guiding us to live in Alignment with God's will.

1 Corinthians 10:13

"No temptation has overtaken you that is not common to man. God is faithful, and he will not let you be tempted beyond your ability, but with the temptation, he will also provide the way of escape, that you may be able to endure it."

Through consistent engagement with Scripture, believers find the strength and clarity to resist temptation and rely on God's faithfulness.

Romans 10:17

"So, faith comes from hearing, and hearing through the word of Christ."

Faith grows as we immerse ourselves in the truth of God's Word, allowing it to shape our understanding and deepen our trust in Him.

Psalm 1:1-3

"Blessed is the man who walks not in the counsel of the wicked, nor stands in the way of sinners, nor sits in the seat of scoffers, but his delight is in the law of the Lord, and on his law, he meditates day and night. He is like a tree planted by streams of water that yields its fruit in its season, and its leaf does not wither."

This passage portrays the transformative power of staying connected to God's Word, likening the believer to a fruitful tree nourished by the life-giving waters of Scripture.

1 Peter 5:7-10

"Casting all your anxieties on him because he cares for you. Be sober-minded; be watchful. Your adversary, the devil, prowls around like a roaring lion. Resist him, firm in your faith... After you have suffered a little while, the God of all grace... will restore, confirm, strengthen, and establish you."

Staying grounded in Scripture enables believers to cast their burdens on God and find the strength to resist the devil's schemes.

James 4:7-10

"Submit yourselves therefore to God. Resist the devil, and he will flee from you. Draw near to God, and he will draw near to you."

By humbling ourselves before God and drawing close to Him through His Word, we find the courage to resist evil and the assurance of His presence.

Ephesians 6:11

"Put on the whole armor of God, that you may be able to stand against the schemes of the devil."

The Word of God is central to the believer's armor, equipping them to face spiritual battles with confidence and resolve.

John 1:1

"In the beginning was the Word, and the Word was with God, and the Word was God."

Jesus, as the living Word, is the foundation of our faith and the source of our strength. Abiding in Him keeps us spiritually steadfast.

Isaiah 35:3-4

"Strengthen the weak hands, and make firm the feeble knees. Say to those who have an anxious heart, 'Be strong; fear not! Behold, your God will come... He will come and save you.'"

The Word provides encouragement and hope, reminding us of God's promise to deliver and sustain His people.

Reflection Questions

Reflection: What obstacles prevent you from maintaining a consistent prayer life?

Action: Set aside a dedicated time daily for prayer and explore new prayer techniques, such as journaling or meditative prayer.

Reflection: How do you currently discern God's guidance in your life?

Action: Practice moments of silence and reflection each day, asking God for clarity and learning to trust His timing.

Reflection: In what ways does worship help you align your heart with God's will

----

Action: Incorporate worship into your week, whether through song, prayer, or acts of service, and reflect on its impact.

Reflection: How can you intentionally embrace rest as part of your relationship with God?

Action: Commit to a Sabbath day or period of rest weekly, focusing on renewal and reconnecting with God.

Reflection: How often do you study Scripture, and how does it shape your daily decisions?

Action: Choose a daily reading plan or devotional to deepen your understanding of God's Word and its application in your life.

Chapter Six
Thriving Through Challenges

Life is often unpredictable and filled with challenges that test our strength and determination. Yet, resilience is the essential quality that enables us to endure these trials and emerge stronger and more adaptable. Resilience is not about avoiding difficulties but facing them head-on with grace and fortitude. In this discussion, we delve into the 7 Cs of resilience—competence, confidence, connection, character, contribution, coping, and control—key principles that provide a roadmap for thriving through adversity.

Life's challenges often feel like a refining fire—a crucible that tests our resolve, reshapes our character, and forges resilience. These trials, though daunting, serve a purpose: to strip away what holds us back and reveal the strength, clarity, and potential within. Much like precious metals are purified in intense heat, adversity refines us, teaching us to rise stronger and more purposeful.

The refining fire doesn't just burn away weaknesses; it illuminates our strengths. It reminds us that hardship is not the end but the beginning of transformation. When the heat feels unbearable, we uncover hidden reserves of courage and endurance in those moments. We learn to trust the process, knowing that growth often comes through discomfort.

Every trial we face becomes a tool in shaping who we are and who we aspire to be. The scars we carry tell stories of survival and resilience, each mark a testament to the refining fire that transformed us. So, when faced with the flames of adversity, embrace them not as destruction but as an opportunity to emerge brighter, stronger, and more refined than ever before.

Understanding Resilience: The Foundation for Thriving

Resilience is the ability to adapt, persevere, and recover from life's setbacks. It involves a combination of emotional, mental, and psychological strengths that enable individuals to maintain optimism, regulate emotions, and solve problems effectively. Resilience isn't about denying hardships but embracing them, learning from them, and remaining hopeful. It recognizes that adversity is part of life but does not define who we are. Through resilience, we harness inner strength, build support networks, and develop strategies to navigate life's challenges with purpose.

The Cs of Resilience: Principles for Thriving Through Challenges

Competence: Building a Foundation of Skills

Resilience begins with competence—the ability to develop and refine the skills needed to face life's challenges. By adopting a growth mindset, continuously learning, and embracing opportunities for self-improvement, you strengthen your capacity to adapt and thrive. Activities that challenge you to think critically and solve problems build the adaptability needed for resilience.

Confidence: Fostering Self-Belief

Confidence is the belief in one's ability to overcome obstacles. It is nurtured by recognizing achievements, celebrating successes, and reframing setbacks as growth opportunities. By fostering a positive self-image and embracing a mindset of perseverance, one can face life's challenges with unwavering assurance.

Connection: Leveraging the Power of Relationships

Strong connections with others are vital for resilience. A supportive family, friends, or mentors network provides empathy, understanding, and perspective during tough times. Building meaningful relationships offers emotional support and exposes you to diverse coping strategies, helping you navigate adversity more effectively.

Character: Anchoring in Values and Integrity

The character represents the moral compass that guides your actions during challenging times. Resilient individuals are rooted in integrity, empathy, and perseverance. By aligning your actions with your core values, you can navigate obstacles with dignity and maintain inner strength, even in adversity.

Contribution: Cultivating Purpose and Meaning

Finding purpose in life is a powerful motivator during difficult times. Engaging in activities that positively impact others—such as volunteering or pursuing a passion—nurtures a sense of fulfillment and purpose. When you focus on contributing to something greater than yourself, you build resilience by creating a deeper connection to your life's meaning.

Coping: Developing Healthy Strategies

Effective coping mechanisms are essential for managing stress and adversity. Practices like Mindfulness, journaling, physical activity, and seeking professional support enable emotional regulation and mental clarity. Healthy coping strategies help you navigate challenges with resilience and balance.

Control: Focusing on What You Can Influence

Resilience involves recognizing what is within your control and letting go of what is not. By focusing your energy on actions, you can take and adapting your mindset to accept uncontrollable elements, you build the strength to face adversity. Ownership of your decisions and reactions empowers you to overcome obstacles and thrive.

Applying the 7 Cs to Thrive Through Challenges

To thrive through life's challenges, integrate the 7 Cs into your daily life:

- Competence: Embrace opportunities to learn and grow, refining skills that align with your goals.
- Confidence: Celebrate achievements and view setbacks as stepping stones for growth.
- Connection: Nurture supportive relationships and foster a sense of community.

- Character: Reflect on your values and act honestly, even in tough times.
- Contribution: Engage in meaningful activities that provide a sense of purpose.
- Coping: Develop healthy habits to manage stress effectively.
- Control: Focus on what you can influence and let go of the rest.

By applying these principles, you cultivate resilience and transform challenges into opportunities for growth and self-discovery, enabling you to thrive no matter the circumstances.

How challenges refine character and faith (zechariah 13:9).

This prophecy reveals that undergoing trials and refinement is an essential path for believers in God to achieve salvation. Only by experiencing God's work of purification can our inner corruption be cleansed. Through this process, our faith, love, and understanding of God are strengthened, enabling us to develop genuine reverence and adoration for Him.

As one passage eloquently states: "The truth is not inherently possessed by man, and is not easily understood by those who Satan has corrupted; man is devoid of the truth and devoid of the resolve to put the truth into practice, and if he does not suffer, and is not refined or judged, then his resolve will never be made perfect. For all people, refinement is excruciating and very difficult to accept—yet it is during refinement that God makes plain His righteous disposition to man, makes public His requirements for man, and provides more enlightenment and more actual pruning and dealing through the comparison between the facts and the truth, He gives man a greater knowledge of himself and the truth, and gives man a greater understanding of God's will, thus allowing man to have a truer and purer love of God. Such are God's aims in carrying out refinement."

These words demonstrate that trials and refinements are meticulously arranged by God to help us grow in character and faith. Like ore that is transformed into quality steel through intense tempering, we, too, must endure the refining fire to become stronger and more aligned with God's purpose. As Zechariah 13:9 illustrates, challenges refine our character and deepen our faith, allowing us to shed corruption and recognize God's profound love and wisdom. When we face these trials with the courage of the apostles and prophets, we gain a clearer understanding of God's will and a heart that truly loves Him.

Choosing Gratitude in Trials

Life is filled with trials that challenge us, but how we respond to them is far more important than the trials themselves. The Bible offers profound guidance on this subject, urging us to "count it all joy" when faced with difficulties (James 1:2). But what does this mean in practice? Let's explore the depth of this teaching and its transformative power through the lens of gratitude.

The Significance of Joy Amid Trials

At first glance, James 1:2's call to "count it all joy" may seem paradoxical. Trials are often accompanied by pain and uncertainty, so how can joy coexist with suffering? The key lies in understanding the difference between happiness and joy. Happiness is fleeting, often dependent on external circumstances, while joy is a steadfast contentment rooted in faith and trust in God.

James 1:3-4 explains that trials serve a divine purpose: "The testing of your faith produces steadfastness. And let steadfastness have its full effect, that you may be perfect and complete, lacking in nothing." Trials refine our character, much like fire purifies gold, shaping us into more patient, compassionate, and humble individuals.

Moreover, choosing joy during trials is a powerful testament to our faith. When others see us maintaining joy and gratitude in adversity, it opens the door to sharing our hope in Christ. As 1 Peter 3:15 reminds us, we must be ready to explain this hope to those who ask.

The Role of Gratitude in Embracing Trials

Gratitude is the bridge that helps us align our hearts with God's perspective during trials. Choosing gratitude does not mean ignoring pain or pretending everything is fine; it means acknowledging God's goodness and sovereignty even in hardship.

1. Gratitude Shifts Our Perspective

By practicing gratitude, we redirect our focus from what we lack to what we have. This shift allows us to recognize God's blessings, no matter how small, fostering a sense of joy. For instance, even in times of loss or struggle, we can thank God for His presence, promises, and provision.

2. Gratitude Cultivates Trust in God

Trials often bring feelings of helplessness. By surrendering control and expressing gratitude, we acknowledge that God is working all things for our good (Romans 8:28). This trust transforms our perspective, enabling us to find peace and even joy amid uncertainty.

3. Gratitude Strengthens Endurance

James links joy with perseverance, emphasizing that endurance leads to spiritual maturity. Gratitude fuels this process by keeping our focus on God's faithfulness, helping us endure trials with hope and strength.

Biblical Examples of Gratitude in Suffering

The Bible provides inspiring examples of individuals who chose joy and gratitude in the face of trials:

Paul and Silas: After being beaten and imprisoned, they sang hymns of praise to God (Acts 16:25). Their gratitude led to their deliverance and the salvation of others.

Job: Despite losing everything, Job declared, "The Lord gave, and the Lord has taken away; blessed be the name of the Lord" (Job 1:21). His unwavering gratitude revealed his deep trust in God.

Jesus: Hebrews 12:2 tells us that Jesus endured the cross "for the joy set before him." His willingness to face unimaginable suffering was rooted in gratitude for the salvation it would bring.

Cultivating Joy Through Gratitude

How can we practically choose gratitude in trials? Here are some actionable steps:

Practice Daily Gratitude: Start each day by listing three things you're thankful for, even during tough times. This practice helps cultivate a mindset of thankfulness.

Surround Yourself with Support: Lean on trusted friends, prayer partners, or a community of believers who can encourage you to focus on God's faithfulness.

Surrender Control: Pray for the strength to let go of anxiety and trust God's plan. Remind yourself that He can bring good even from the hardest situations.

Focus on Eternal Perspective: Remember that earthly trials are temporary. Keeping your eyes on eternity can help you endure with joy and gratitude.

Joy, Gratitude, and God's Purpose

Trials are opportunities for growth, faith, and deeper intimacy with God. Choosing joy and gratitude in these moments is not easy, but it is profoundly transformative. As you face challenges, remember the examples of Paul, Job, and Jesus, and embrace the wisdom of James 1:2. Gratitude is not just a response to blessings—it is a deliberate choice to trust God, even when life is hard. In doing so, you'll discover a joy that surpasses understanding and reflects God's glory to those around you.

The first chapter of Philippians offers a profound reflection on gratitude and steadfast faith, especially amidst uncertainty and suffering. The Apostle Paul's deep affection for the believers in Philippi shines through in his letter. His words radiate Encouragement and appreciation for their faith and devotion, even in challenging circumstances. This chapter serves as a testament to the power of gratitude and the transformative impact of living out one's faith.

The Roots of the Philippian Church

The church's origins in Philippi, as recounted in Acts 16, provide a backdrop that enriches our understanding of Paul's gratitude. Despite imprisonment, Paul and Silas demonstrated unwavering faith by singing hymns and praying. Their actions, fueled by a profound trust in God, impacted their fellow prisoners and the jailer, who ultimately surrendered his life to Christ. This moment is a vivid example of how faith in action can lead others to salvation.

Lydia, another pivotal figure in the Philippian church's early days, exemplifies the intersection of prosperity and faith. A successful businesswoman dealing in purple goods, the Lord opened Lydia's heart as Paul preached. Her immediate response—baptism and hospitality—illustrates the fruit of a heart devoted to God. Her likely role in supporting the fledgling church underscores the impact one faithful individual can have on a community.

Paul's Encouragement to the Philippians

Unlike many of Paul's letters, which include admonishments or corrections, Philippians brims with Encouragement. Paul calls the believers to remain steadfast, united, and bold in the face of opposition. His words, "Let your manner of life be worthy of the gospel of Christ" (Philippians 1:27), challenge them to let their faith manifest in both word and action. This exhortation is not a call to earn salvation but an invitation to live out the gospel as a testament to God's transformative power.

Paul's emphasis on standing firm and striving together resonates with other biblical examples of faith in action, such as the crumbling walls of Jericho or David's victory over Goliath. These stories remind us that faith and obedience glorify God and accomplish His purposes.

Lessons for Today

Paul's message to the Philippians remains deeply relevant in a culture that prioritizes self-glorification over humility and service. Society frequently encourages individuals to seek their comfort, image, and success above all else. However, Philippians 1 invites believers to adopt an entirely different perspective—one rooted in gratitude, trust, and a commitment to glorifying God.

This chapter highlights four key truths about God:

God is efficient: He uses every situation, even suffering, for His purposes and our good (Romans 8:28).

God is transcendent: His truth prevails over societal messages and cultural narratives.

God is timely: He acts according to His perfect plan, making a way where there seems to be none.

God is unmovable: His promises are steadfast, and His Word endures forever.

Living with Gratitude and Purpose

As followers of Christ, we are called to embody these attributes—not for self-glorification but to point others to Him. Our attitude of hope and trust, especially in difficult times, can become a powerful testimony of God's goodness and faithfulness. Gratitude, even in trials, reflects a deep-seated confidence in God's sovereignty and purpose.

Paul's example encourages us to see every challenge as an opportunity to grow closer to God and to reflect His glory to the world. When we choose gratitude and faith over fear and self-pity, we allow God to use us as instruments of His love and truth, inspiring others to seek Him.

In this first chapter of Philippians, Paul reminds us that our lives, when rooted in Christ, can be a beacon of hope and a reflection of God's unchanging character. Like the Philippians, we may embrace a life of gratitude and unwavering faith, trusting that God's work in and through us will yield eternal fruit.

Standing Firm in the Storm

Life often feels like a storm—unpredictable, chaotic, and overwhelming. The call to "stand firm" takes on profound significance in these moments. It is not about merely surviving the storm but thriving through it by anchoring ourselves in faith, hope, and unwavering trust in God. Standing firm in the storm is a physical act and a spiritual posture, a testament to God's strength working within us.

Anchoring in Faith

The Apostle Paul's Encouragement to the Philippians offers a powerful example of standing firm. Despite being imprisoned, he writes with joy and gratitude, urging the believers to "let your manner of life be worthy of the gospel of Christ... standing firm in one spirit" (Philippians 1:27). His confidence did not come from his circumstances but from his deep trust in God's sovereignty. Similarly, faith becomes our anchor when the winds of uncertainty blow. Hebrews 11:1 reminds us, "Faith is the assurance of things hoped for, the conviction of things not seen." This assurance allows us to remain unshaken, even when life feels unstable.

Drawing Strength from God

Standing firm does not mean relying on our strength. Instead, it involves surrendering to God's power. Ephesians 6:10-11 reminds us to "be strong in the Lord and the strength of his might. Put on the whole armor of God, that you may be able to stand against the schemes of the devil." Through prayer, Scripture, and the Holy Spirit, we are equipped with divine strength to face the storms of life.

The Testimony of Trials

Storms have a purpose—they refine us and showcase God's glory. James 1:2-3 encourages us to "count it all joy, my brothers when you meet trials of various kinds, for you know that the testing of your faith produces steadfastness." Like Paul and Silas singing in their prison cell (Acts 16), our response to trials can point others to Christ. Standing firm in the storm is not just for our benefit but a powerful witness to God's sustaining grace.

Unity in the Storm

Paul's exhortation to the Philippians highlights the importance of unity: "striving side by side for the faith of the gospel" (Philippians 1:27). Storms often isolate us. Still, we are called to stand firm together. Community strengthens us, providing Encouragement, accountability, and shared faith. When we stand united, we reflect the body of Christ, a beacon of hope in a turbulent world.

Trusting the Calm Beyond

Every storm has an end, even when it feels endless. The disciples learned this lesson when Jesus calmed the sea (Mark 4:39). His words, "Peace! Be still," remind us that God is in control and capable of bringing peace to even the most chaotic situations. Standing firm means trusting that God will bring us through the storm in His perfect timing.

Renewing Your Mind

What does "renewing the mind" look like for Christians? This question often lingers in the hearts of believers, many of whom struggle to grasp its significance due to limited teaching on the subject. The lack of understanding leaves many feeling unfulfilled and confused, unable to fully experience the abundant life Jesus promised in John 10:10 (NLT): "The thief's purpose is to steal and kill and destroy. My purpose is to give them a rich and satisfying life." This abundant life is unlocked through one transformative principle: renewing the mind.

What Does "Renewing of the Mind" Mean?

Renewing your mind, as described in Romans 12:2, is a transformative process in which life is interpreted through the lens of God's Word and the guidance of the Holy Spirit rather than personal experiences, traumas, preferences, or external opinions. It's a paradigm shift—seeing yourself, others, and the world through the perspective of God's Kingdom. This shift involves daily choices to adopt the mind of Christ, which dwells within believers as new creations, rejecting the old, worldly way of thinking.

The Importance of Renewing the Mind

Without a renewed mind, Christians often remain trapped in cycles of defeat, striving in their own strength or waiting for God to intervene without understanding their role in transformation. The Bible emphasizes this renewal as a pathway to Spirit-led power and freedom, moving believers beyond mere religious obligation into lives marked by God's presence and purpose.

Renewal aligns your thoughts with God's truth by identifying and rejecting lies, replacing them with Scripture's promises, and reinforcing these truths. For instance, 2 Corinthians 10:5 (ESV) exhorts believers to "take every thought captive to obey Christ." This means examining thoughts to determine if they align with God's Word. If a thought conflicts with God's promises, it must be rejected and replaced with Scripture, planting seeds of truth that shape beliefs and actions.

The Biblical Foundation of Renewing the Mind

In 2 Peter 1:3-4, Scripture declares that God's divine power equips believers with everything needed for a godly life through knowledge of Him and His promises: "Through these, He has given us His precious and magnificent promises, so that through them you may become partakers of the divine nature..." Embracing these promises allows believers to participate in God's divine nature, escaping worldly corruption.

Renewing the mind enables believers to fuel their lives with godly thoughts and beliefs, creating alignment with God's plans. Proverbs 23:7 (KJV) reinforces this truth: "For as he thinketh in his heart, so is he." Beliefs are shaped by thoughts, which determine actions and boundaries in life.

Renewing the Mind: Spiritual and Physiological Change

This process is not solely spiritual; it has a physiological basis. Science confirms that intentional thought patterns reshape the brain through neuroplasticity. Aligning thoughts with God's Word creates new neural pathways, making Kingdom-focused thinking more natural over time. This transformation facilitates solutions, strategies, and opportunities that align with God's purposes.

Practical Steps for Renewing the Mind

Recognize

Capture each thought and evaluate it against God's Word. Ask, "Does this thought align with God's promises, or is it a lie from the enemy?"

Replace

Replace lies with Scriptures that reflect God's truth. For example, if fear dominates your thoughts, meditate on verses like Isaiah 41:10: "Fear not, for I am with you."

Reinforce

Revisit these truths consistently. Write affirmations, post Scriptures where you'll see them, and declare them daily to strengthen godly beliefs.

Visualize

Use your imagination to envision living out God's promises. Imagine what life looks like when fully aligned with His will, creating agreement between your thoughts and His truth.

Affirm

Speak affirmations based on Scripture to embed God's promises in your heart. For example, declare, "I am a new creation in Christ; the old has gone, and the new has come" (2 Corinthians 5:17).

The Abundant Life Through a Renewed Mind

Transformation becomes inevitable when you commit to renewing your mind, aligning your thoughts with God's Word, and rejecting lies. As this alignment deepens, you'll witness the abundant life Jesus promised unfolding in your circumstances. Doors of opportunity, favor, and blessings appear as you agree with God's design.

Renewing your mind is a daily, intentional journey that invites God's Kingdom to reign, transforming your thoughts, actions, relationships, and destiny.

Replacing negativity with faith-based affirmations involves recognizing harmful thought patterns, realigning them with God's Word, and intentionally reinforcing positive, faith-filled truths. Here's how to do it effectively:

1. Recognize Negative Thoughts

The first step is awareness. Negative thoughts often appear as fear, self-doubt, or discouragement, subtly influencing your perspective. Identify these thoughts by asking:

Does this align with God's promises?

Is this thought uplifting, or does it bring me down?

Scriptural Basis: In 2 Corinthians 10:5 (ESV), Paul teaches, "We destroy arguments and every lofty opinion raised against the knowledge of God, and take every thought captive to obey Christ."

Example:

Negative Thought: "I'm not good enough."

Response: Recognize this as a lie that contradicts God's Word.

2. Replace with Faith-Based Affirmations

Once you identify a negative thought, replace it with a Bible-based truth. This requires anchoring your affirmations in Scripture to align your mind with God's promises.

Steps to Create Affirmations:

Find Scriptures that counteract the negativity.

Turn these Scriptures into personal, positive statements.

Examples of Affirmations:

Negative Thought: "I can't do this."

Affirmation: "I can do all things through Christ who strengthens me" (Philippians 4:13).

Negative Thought: "I'm all alone."

Affirmation: "The Lord is with me; I will not be afraid" (Psalm 118:6).

Negative Thought: "I'm not worthy."

Affirmation: "I am fearfully and wonderfully made" (Psalm 139:14).

3. Reinforce Through Repetition

Faith-based affirmations are most effective when they become a daily habit. Repetition rewires your mind, creating new patterns of thought.

Ways to Reinforce:

Write and Display: Place affirmations on sticky notes or cards in visible places like your bathroom mirror or workspace.

Speak Aloud: Declare affirmations daily with confidence and faith. Hearing your voice strengthens their impact.

Incorporate Prayer: Include affirmations in your prayers, asking the Holy Spirit to root them in your heart.

4. Visualize Your Affirmations

God has given us an imagination to help us align with His will. Visualizing what life looks like when living in these truths can strengthen your faith.

Imagine walking confidently, trusting God's provision, or overcoming obstacles through His strength.

Combine visualization with affirmations for a deeper connection to the promises of God.

Scriptural Basis: "Now to him who can do immeasurably more than all we ask or imagine, according to his power at work within us" (Ephesians 3:20).

5. Anchor Affirmations in Gratitude and Faith

Faith-based affirmations are more powerful when rooted in gratitude and belief. Thank God for His promises as if they are already fulfilled, reinforcing your trust in Him.

Example Prayer:

"Lord, I thank You for allowing me to do all things through Christ. I praise You for Your strength and guidance in my life, and I declare that I will walk in Your power today."

6. Persist Despite Opposition

Negative thoughts may reappear, but persistence is key. Repeat your affirmations whenever a negative thought arises and lean into God's Word.

Scriptural Encouragement: "Do not be conformed to this world, but be transformed by the renewal of your mind" (Romans 12:2).

Faith-Based Affirmations You Can Start With:

"God has not given me a spirit of fear but of power, love, and self-control" (2 Timothy 1:7).

"I am more than a conqueror through Him who loves me" (Romans 8:37).

"The Lord will fight for me; I need only to be still" (Exodus 14:14).

"God's plans for me are good, to give me hope and a future" (Jeremiah 29:11).

"I am God's masterpiece, created in Christ Jesus to do good works" (Ephesians 2:10).

You can transform negative thought patterns into faith-filled confidence by consistently recognizing, replacing, reinforcing, visualizing, and affirming God's promises.

Embracing Change As Growth

Change is an inevitable part of life, manifesting through unexpected events or intentional decisions. Instead of fearing or resisting it, we can view change as a powerful catalyst for personal growth. By embracing the challenges and opportunities it presents, we unlock pathways for self-discovery, learning, and development. Embracing change allows us to grow beyond our limitations and embark on a transformative journey toward realizing our fullest potential.

The Power of Change in Shaping Growth

Change is a constant force that influences and shapes every aspect of our lives. It challenges us to adapt, evolve, and step beyond our comfort zones. When we accept change, we open ourselves to opportunities that broaden our perspectives and enrich our personal development. From strengthening relationships to advancing careers, embracing change propels growth across all areas of life, enabling us to become more resilient, adaptable, and self-aware.

Recognizing the Need for Growth

Personal growth is a lifelong journey of improvement and evolution. Acknowledging the need for growth signals an openness to learning and self-improvement. This awareness allows us to leverage change as a transformative tool, converting challenges into stepping stones for development. By embracing change, we can harness its power to refine our skills, expand our knowledge, and nurture a mindset that thrives on continuous improvement.

The Interplay Between Change and Personal Development

Change and personal development are inherently interconnected. Embracing change introduces us to new experiences, perspectives, and opportunities that stimulate growth. It pushes us to confront fears, overcome insecurities, and develop resilience. Each challenge navigated through change strengthens our self-awareness and equips us with the tools to adapt to future uncertainties. Through this process, we cultivate a deeper understanding of ourselves and our potential, fostering ongoing personal development.

Benefits of Embracing Change

1. Broader Perspectives and Open-mindedness

Accepting change enables us to explore diverse viewpoints and gain fresh insights. This openness enriches our understanding of the world and enhances empathy, creativity, and problem-solving abilities, paving the way for more meaningful interactions and effective decisions.

2. Enhanced Resilience and Adaptability

Navigating through change builds our capacity to adapt to unfamiliar situations and recover from setbacks. This resilience fosters confidence in managing uncertainties, ensuring we remain grounded and proactive in adversity.

3. Heightened Self-awareness

Embracing change prompts self-reflection, encouraging us to examine our values, beliefs, and behaviors. This introspection identifies areas for improvement, enabling intentional growth and informed decision-making.

4. Improved Problem-solving Skills

Change often requires innovative thinking and decision-making. By facing new challenges head-on, we cultivate the ability to devise creative solutions, making us more resourceful and adaptable in both personal and professional spheres.

Strategies for Embracing Change as Growth

1. Cultivate a Growth Mindset

A growth mindset views change as an opportunity to learn and grow. This perspective transforms challenges into valuable experiences and fosters optimism, curiosity, and resilience.

2. Embrace Discomfort and Uncertainty

Growth requires stepping outside of our comfort zones. By accepting discomfort as part of the process, we build the strength to navigate uncertainties and expand our capabilities.

3. Set Realistic Goals and Take Action

Goal-setting provides direction during periods of change. By breaking larger objectives into achievable steps, we maintain focus and momentum, ensuring steady progress toward personal growth.

4. Seek Support and Collaborate

Engaging with mentors, peers, or support networks helps us navigate change with guidance and Encouragement. Collaborative learning fosters mutual growth, making the journey more enriching.

5. Practice Self-compassion

Change can be challenging, and setbacks are inevitable. Practicing kindness and understanding toward ourselves helps us stay motivated and embrace the learning process without undue self-criticism.

Overcoming Barriers to Growth

Fear of the Unknown

The uncertainty that accompanies change can be daunting. Reframing this fear as an opportunity for exploration helps us approach the unknown with excitement and curiosity.

Comfort Zone Limitations

While familiarity offers security, growth requires venturing beyond it. Recognizing the potential for transformation outside our comfort zones empowers us to embrace change with courage.

Self-doubt

Believing in our capacity to learn and grow counteracts the limiting effects of self-doubt. Celebrating small achievements builds confidence and reinforces our ability to embrace change effectively.

Embracing Change as Growth

Change provides opportunities to explore new possibilities, learn from past experiences, and expand our knowledge and skills. It equips us with the resilience and emotional intelligence needed to navigate life's complexities. By embracing change, we nurture personal development and create a foundation for lifelong growth.

In conclusion, change is a challenge and a profound opportunity for transformation. Viewing it through the lens of growth allows us to uncover our potential and thrive in life's uncertainties. So, leap—embrace change and let it propel you toward personal growth and fulfillment.

Change is an inevitable part of life, constantly influencing our journey. Transitions often bring excitement and uncertainty, whether starting a new job, ending a relationship, or relocating to a new city. By adopting the right mindset and strategies, we can navigate these shifts gracefully and emerge stronger.

Acceptance as the Foundation

The first step to navigating change is acknowledging that it is a natural part of life. Instead of resisting or denying it, approach change with openness and curiosity. Acceptance doesn't require you to enjoy every aspect of the transition, but it helps you move forward with clarity and purpose.

Building Resilience

Resilience—recovering from challenges—is key to thriving during transitions. Cultivate resilience by developing coping strategies, practicing self-care, and leaning on supportive relationships. Focusing on your strengths can also empower you to face difficulties with confidence.

Welcoming Uncertainty

Transitions often involve the unknown, which can feel daunting. Instead of fearing uncertainty, view it as a gateway to growth and exploration. Use this time to develop new skills, meet new people, and uncover hidden passions. Embracing the unknown can lead to opportunities you might not have considered.

Adopting Flexibility

Rigid thinking can make adapting to change more difficult. Instead, stay flexible and open to new ideas, perspectives, and opportunities that arise. Flexibility allows you to adjust your approach when necessary, making it easier to navigate through transitions.

Controlling the Controllable

While many aspects of change are beyond your influence, focus on what you can control. Proactively manage your reactions, emotions, and actions during transitions. Concentrating on areas within your control allows you to maintain a sense of empowerment and agency.

Practicing Mindfulness

Mindfulness—being present and nonjudgmental—can help you stay grounded during periods of change. Engage in practices like meditation, deep breathing, or journaling to foster Mindfulness. These techniques can enhance your perspective and keep you centered amidst uncertainty.

Seeking Support

You don't have to face transitions alone. Turn to friends, family, or professional counselors for guidance and Encouragement. Building a strong support network can provide reassurance and help you navigate challenges more effectively.

Celebrating Milestones

As you transition, take time to acknowledge and celebrate your progress. Recognizing small victories reinforces your resilience and reminds you of your ability to overcome obstacles.

Navigating life's transitions with grace involves embracing acceptance, cultivating resilience, remaining flexible, and practicing Mindfulness. By welcoming change with the right strategies, you can approach transitions confidently and use them as opportunities for growth. Remember, change is not an adversary but a catalyst for transformation. By embracing it, you'll be better equipped to handle whatever comes your way.

Reflection Questions

Reflection: How have challenges in your life refined your character and deepened your faith? Reflect on Zechariah 13:9, where trials are compared to a refining fire.

Action: Identify a recent challenge and journal about how it shaped you positively.

Reflection: How can gratitude shift your perspective during adversity?

Action: Start a gratitude journal, listing three things you're thankful for each day, even during trials.

Reflection: Reflect on the parable of the house on the rock (Matthew 7:24-27). What foundations in your life help you stand firm during storms?

Action: Strengthen your spiritual foundation through prayer, scripture reading, or connecting with a faith community.

Reflection: What negative thoughts do you need to replace with faith-based affirmations?

Action: Create a list of affirmations grounded in faith to counteract negativity and repeat them daily.

Reflection: How can you view change as an opportunity for growth rather than a threat?

Action: Write down one area of change in your life and list three ways it could help you grow.

Chapter Seven
Celebrating The Journey

If you're anything like me, celebrating your achievements doesn't come naturally. Success often feels like a moving target—the closer you get, the further it seems to drift away. But the truth is, that ever-shifting benchmark isn't a mirage. It's a reflection of how we see ourselves.

Recently, I completed the second draft of my second novel, a milestone I had been working toward all summer. Finishing it should have felt monumental—a moment worthy of celebration. Yet, as I closed my laptop, the accomplishment felt strangely underwhelming. To be fair, the chaos of current events had left me feeling stressed and preoccupied, which may have dampened my mood. Even so, I knew I couldn't let the moment pass without acknowledging it.

So, I took a small step. I texted some writer friends to share the news and decided to write this blog post. Hearing "congratulations" from friends made the achievement feel more real. Sharing the milestone, even simply, reminded me that celebrating success is just as important as working toward it.

The Perfectionist Trap

One of the things I struggle with is how often I downplay my accomplishments. My inner perfectionist sets impossibly high standards, which makes it easy to breeze past milestones without a second thought. For instance, good grades became an expectation rather than a reason to celebrate in college. Similarly, as a writer, I see finishing drafts and sharing my work as basic requirements for success—not milestones worthy of recognition.

But here's the danger: if you constantly raise the bar without pausing to celebrate, you may spend your entire life feeling like you're never good enough. While it's healthy to challenge yourself and strive for growth, it's equally important to honor the progress you've made along the way.

How to Celebrate Your Achievements

If you find pausing and celebrating success uncomfortable, you're not alone. To help you break the cycle, here are a few ideas for marking those important moments, big or small:

Treat Yourself: Indulge in something small but meaningful—a pint of Ben & Jerry's, a coffee from your favorite café, or a bouquet of fresh flowers. It doesn't have to be extravagant; what matters is taking a moment to reward yourself.

Have a Spa Night: Run a bubble bath, wear a face mask, and relax with soothing music. It's a simple way to unwind and acknowledge your hard work.

Take a Mini Adventure: A short road trip or even a visit to a local park can provide a refreshing change of scenery. Sometimes, stepping away from your usual surroundings is the best way to reflect on your journey.

Plan a Movie Night: Cook your favorite meal or order takeout, then settle in for a cozy night with a good film. Invite friends or enjoy some alone time—the choice is yours.

Buy Something You've Wanted: Reward yourself with a thoughtful purchase. After finishing my first draft, I treated myself to laptop stickers I had been eyeing for months.

Share Your Achievement: Call or text a friend to tell them what you've accomplished. Having someone else celebrate with you can make the milestone more tangible and meaningful.

Go for a Reflective Walk: Put on your favorite playlist, head outside, and take some time to reflect on your journey. Use this moment to cheer yourself on—you've earned it!

Plan a Fun Activity: Organize something special, whether it's a picnic, hiking trip, museum visit, or trying out a new hobby. Celebrating doesn't have to look the same every time; make it personal and enjoyable.

Embracing the Journey

Success isn't just about reaching the destination—it's about appreciating the steps that got you there. By taking the time to celebrate your wins, you'll not only honor your hard work but also build the resilience and motivation to keep going. So, don't let it go unnoticed next time you hit a goal. Celebrate it, even if it feels uncomfortable. You deserve it.

Recognizing Milestones

Recognizing and celebrating milestones is a powerful tool for boosting team morale, motivation, and overall satisfaction. Acknowledging achievements highlights team members' hard work and dedication, fostering a positive work culture. By celebrating milestones, teams can cultivate a sense of accomplishment, promote collaboration, and inspire ongoing success.

This guide outlines steps to effectively recognize and celebrate team milestones, project completions, or successful outcomes, aligning these celebrations with the core values of recognition and appreciation.

Step 1: Define the Milestone

Begin by clearly identifying the milestone to be celebrated. Whether completing a major project, meeting a significant goal, or achieving a notable outcome, ensure it is well-defined, measurable, and aligned with the team's objectives. This clarity reinforces the achievement's importance and sets the stage for meaningful recognition.

Step 2: Plan the Celebration

Once the milestone is defined, plan a celebration that resonates with the team. Tailor the activity to team preferences and interests, such as team lunches, happy hours, recognition ceremonies, or off-site events. Consider the milestone's significance, the resources available, and the team dynamic when determining the celebration's budget, location, and duration.

Step 3: Communicate the Achievement

Before the celebration, communicate the milestone to the team and relevant stakeholders. Use team meetings, emails, or dedicated communication channels to highlight the accomplishment's significance. Recognize the efforts of individuals and the team, expressing gratitude for their contributions. This step ensures everyone feels included and aware of the success being celebrated.

Step 4: Celebrate as a Team

Gather the team to commemorate the milestone. Create an atmosphere of excitement and positivity by reflecting on the journey, emphasizing challenges overcome, and lessons learned. Recognize individual and collective contributions while encouraging team members to share their experiences. This fosters a sense of unity and camaraderie, strengthening team bonds.

Step 5: Express Appreciation

During the celebration, express genuine appreciation for the team's dedication and hard work. Use personalized messages, certificates, or small tokens of recognition to highlight individual achievements. Acknowledging specific contributions and their impact reinforces a culture of appreciation, motivating the team to maintain momentum.

Key Considerations When Recognizing Milestones

Timing

Recognize milestones promptly to maintain their significance. This includes acknowledging major events, like anniversaries or product launches, and smaller project milestones to instill a culture of continuous recognition.

Visibility and Inclusivity

Ensure celebrations are visible and inclusive across the organization. Recognition from senior leadership, especially when tied to company values, enhances its impact. Use diverse communication channels to ensure every team member feels part of the celebration regardless of location or time zone.

Personalization

Personalized recognition is the most impactful. Highlight how achievements align with organizational values and individuals' tangible contributions. Tailoring celebrations to the milestone's context ensures relevance and sincerity.

Authenticity

Authentic celebrations that reflect the organization's culture are more meaningful and enduring. Encourage managers to personalize team milestone celebrations, adding a unique and genuine touch.

Ideas for Celebrating Milestones

Gratitude and Recognition: Publicly acknowledge achievements through senior leadership messages, either in person, via video, or on internal platforms.

Gatherings: Host virtual or in-person events like happy hours or mini-conferences for teams to socialize and celebrate collectively.

Highlight Achievements: Use newsletters, press releases, or communication channels to showcase the milestone and recognize contributors.

Tokens of Appreciation: Distribute personalized gifts or company-branded items to commemorate the occasion.

Special Spaces: Dedicate a virtual or physical workspace to honor the milestone and the team.

Learning Opportunities: Offer professional development resources, such as workshops or online courses, as a reward.

Incentives: Provide special rewards tied to the milestone, like discounts, bonuses, or company-wide perks.

Anniversary Celebrations: Mark significant events, such as product launches or company anniversaries, to reinforce shared accomplishments.

The Value of Celebrating Milestones

Recognizing and celebrating milestones is not just about marking achievements; it reinforces the importance of perseverance, hard work, and collaboration. It ensures employees feel valued, engaged, and motivated while fostering a culture of excellence. By linking milestone recognition to organizational values, leaders can inspire continued dedication and align team efforts with long-term goals.

Through thoughtful and inclusive celebrations, organizations create memorable experiences that energize teams and build a foundation for sustained success.

Not all milestones are created equal, but many moments within a team or organization deserve recognition. Identifying these moments requires understanding their significance to the team's objectives, values, and morale. Below are strategies to help pinpoint achievements worth celebrating:

1. Link Milestones to Organizational Goals

Consider whether the milestone directly contributes to the team's or organization's objectives. For instance:

Completing a critical project that impacts the company's bottom line.

Achieving or surpassing key performance indicators (KPIs) like revenue targets, customer satisfaction scores, or sales milestones.

By tying celebrations to meaningful goals, you ensure that recognition reinforces the team's sense of purpose and alignment with the organization's mission.

2. Recognize Growth and Progress

Celebrating progress is essential for building momentum, even if it doesn't represent a final result. Look for:

Milestones in ongoing projects include reaching a halfway point or clearing significant hurdles.

Team or individual growth, like mastering a new skill, completing training, or adapting to new challenges.

These moments help reinforce the idea that incremental progress is valuable and worthy of acknowledgment.

3. Celebrate Overcoming Challenges

When a team works through adversity or succeeds despite significant obstacles, that effort is worth celebrating. Examples include:

Recovering a project that was behind schedule.

Adapting successfully to unexpected challenges, such as tight deadlines or resource constraints.

Acknowledging these achievements builds resilience and confidence.

4. Mark Organizational and Team Milestones

Celebrate events that highlight the team's journey or the organization's growth, such as:

Anniversaries of the company, team formation, or a product launch.

Expanding into a new market, opening new offices, or launching innovative products.

These moments reinforce a shared sense of history and accomplishment.

5. Highlight Individual Contributions

While team achievements are important, individual accomplishments also deserve recognition. Examples include:

Employees who demonstrate exceptional performance or go above and beyond.

Individuals who embody the organization's core values in their work.

Celebrating these moments encourages others to emulate exemplary behavior.

6. Acknowledge Collaborative Success

A team successfully collaborates across departments or with external partners signifies a noteworthy milestone. Celebrate instances such as:

Cross-functional teams working together seamlessly on a major initiative.

Successful partnerships with clients or vendors that result in shared success.

These celebrations reinforce collaboration and teamwork as core principles.

7. Pay Attention to Employee Well-being

Sometimes, moments worth celebrating aren't tied to performance metrics but to the well-being and morale of the team. Consider celebrating:

Personal milestones, like birthdays, work anniversaries, or promotions.

Acts of kindness include a team member stepping in to support others during challenging times.

Leaders create an inclusive and supportive environment by celebrating humanity within the workplace.

8. Identify Moments of Innovation

Innovation deserves recognition, whether it's a breakthrough idea, a streamlined process, or a creative problem-solving approach. Celebrate:

Initiatives that save time reduce costs or improve efficiency.

Creative contributions that bring fresh perspectives to a project or challenge.

Acknowledging innovation fosters a culture of creativity and continuous improvement.

Gratitude in Success

Gratitude is a transformative emotion that can profoundly influence your well-being, success, and happiness. By recognizing and appreciating the positive aspects of life, gratitude fosters a mindset that promotes optimism, strengthens connections, and builds resilience. When integrated into daily routines, gratitude reshapes how individuals approach challenges and seize opportunities. Its ripple effects extend to personal and professional realms, acting as a catalyst for creating nurturing, positive environments. Below, we explore how gratitude contributes to success and happiness in various dimensions of life.

Gratitude and Mental Well-Being

Focusing on gratitude shifts attention away from stress and negativity, reducing anxiety, depression, and emotional overwhelm. Research indicates that individuals who practice gratitude regularly experience increased happiness and lower stress levels. This emotional recalibration improves mental health and equips individuals with a more positive outlook, enabling them to tackle life's difficulties with greater resilience.

Gratitude in Relationships

Gratitude enriches relationships by fostering mutual respect, trust, and appreciation. When people acknowledge the contributions of others—whether colleagues, friends, or family—they strengthen their social bonds. Expressing gratitude professionally can enhance teamwork and collaboration, creating an atmosphere where respect and shared goals flourish. For instance, a leader who appreciates their team's efforts cultivates loyalty and motivation, paving the way for personal and collective achievements.

Resilience and Growth through Gratitude

One of gratitude's most powerful effects is its ability to bolster resilience. In the face of challenges, a grateful perspective highlights opportunities for growth and learning rather than focusing solely on setbacks. This positive framing fosters perseverance and hope, enabling individuals to recover from adversity and maintain progress toward long-term success.

Gratitude as a Productivity Driver

In professional and personal settings, gratitude boosts motivation by encouraging recognition of one's progress and available resources. This recognition drives commitment to goals, increases energy levels, and fosters a sense of purpose. Employees who feel appreciated are more productive, while individuals who acknowledge their milestones feel inspired to strive further. In this way, gratitude is a cornerstone for enhanced performance and achievement.

Cultivating a Gratitude-Focused Mindset

Gratitude trains the brain to focus on the positive, fostering a mindset that enhances self-esteem, optimism, and a sense of purpose. This mental shift supports continuous personal growth and goal attainment. For example, maintaining a gratitude journal—recording three things to be grateful for daily—can improve happiness and life satisfaction. Individuals maintain momentum and positivity in their endeavors by celebrating even small victories.

Gratitude in Leadership and Collaboration

Leaders who embody gratitude create trust, respect, and psychological safety environments. Acknowledging team members' efforts enhances morale and strengthens collaboration and innovation. In such settings, gratitude nurtures a collective sense of purpose, fostering productivity and success at every organizational level.

Gratitude in Adversity

Even during challenging times, gratitude serves as a powerful ally. Individuals can shift their perspective, uncover silver linings, and maintain resilience by identifying aspects to be thankful for. For instance, viewing setbacks as opportunities to learn or grow transforms obstacles into stepping stones for success.

Expressing Gratitude for a Brighter Future

Active expressions of gratitude—through words, gestures, or thoughtful actions—strengthen connections and foster community. Leaders and individuals can harness this practice to inspire growth, motivate teams, and create a supportive atmosphere. For businesses, gratitude extended to customers solidifies loyalty and shapes a positive brand image, ensuring sustained success.

In summary, gratitude is a pivotal element of success, offering a foundation for mental well-being, strengthened relationships, and personal growth. By adopting gratitude as a core practice, individuals and organizations unlock their full potential, achieving holistic well-being and creating ripples of positivity that enrich every aspect of life. Whether through reflective practices, leadership initiatives, or simple acts of kindness, gratitude illuminates the path to a brighter, more fulfilling future.

Gratitude plays a pivotal role in sustaining growth by fostering resilience, enhancing motivation, and creating a positive environment conducive to continuous development. It serves as a cornerstone for personal, professional, and organizational advancement, shaping the mindset and behaviors needed to navigate challenges and embrace growth opportunities. Below, we explore how gratitude contributes to sustained growth across various dimensions.

1. Strengthening Resilience for Growth

Gratitude encourages a mindset focusing on what is positive and valuable, even in adversity. Individuals and organizations can cultivate resilience by appreciating small victories and recognizing the lessons embedded in setbacks. This resilience enables them to recover quickly from failures, adapt to change, and maintain momentum. For example, reflecting on past successes and support systems during tough times can instill confidence and provide the emotional strength necessary to persevere.

2. Fostering Motivation and Engagement

Gratitude enhances intrinsic motivation by reinforcing a sense of purpose and appreciation. When individuals acknowledge their progress, resources, and the contributions of others, they are more likely to remain committed to their goals. In professional settings, leaders who express gratitude to their teams create an environment where employees feel valued, leading to higher engagement and productivity. This sustained motivation drives consistent effort, which is critical for long-term growth.

3. Building Positive Relationships

Growth often depends on collaboration and strong interpersonal connections. Gratitude strengthens these relationships by fostering trust, mutual respect, and cooperation. Recognizing and appreciating each member's contributions in team settings encourages a culture of support and shared success. Such environments promote psychological safety, empowering individuals to innovate, take risks, and grow together.

4. Encouraging a Growth-Oriented Mindset

Gratitude shifts focus from what is lacking to what is present, helping individuals maintain a mindset that embraces learning and self-improvement. This positive outlook encourages people to see challenges as growth opportunities rather than insurmountable obstacles. For instance, gratitude practices such as journaling or reflection on achievements can help individuals identify areas for development while maintaining a hopeful perspective.

5. Creating a Culture of Appreciation

In organizations, gratitude fuels a culture that prioritizes recognition and appreciation. Such cultures are more likely to retain talent, inspire loyalty, and drive innovation. Employees who feel appreciated are likelier to invest in their roles and contribute to the organization's growth. Moreover, expressing gratitude to customers and stakeholders builds trust and fosters long-term relationships, laying a foundation for sustained success.

6. Enhancing Emotional and Psychological Well-Being

Sustained growth requires a stable emotional foundation. Gratitude supports mental well-being by reducing stress and anxiety, increasing happiness, and fostering optimism. This emotional stability allows individuals to focus on their goals with clarity and determination. For instance, gratitude meditation or mindfulness exercises can improve emotional regulation, ensuring consistent performance and progress.

7. Facilitating Long-Term Vision

Gratitude encourages reflection on past achievements and present opportunities, which helps set a long-term vision. By appreciating the resources, relationships, and milestones that have contributed to current success, individuals and organizations can better plan for future growth. This reflective practice ensures that growth strategies are rooted in a deep understanding of strengths and opportunities.

8. Inspiring Leadership and Influence

Leaders who practice and model gratitude inspire their teams and foster a sense of belonging. Acknowledging contributions and celebrating milestones, they cultivate an environment where individuals are motivated to excel and collaborate. This leadership style not only drives personal growth within teams but also ensures the collective advancement of the organization.

Sharing Your Testimony

Sharing your testimony is a powerful way to inspire others, build connections, and reflect on your journey. Whether your testimony concerns personal growth, overcoming challenges, or achieving success, sharing it can uplift others and solidify your understanding of your experiences. Below are key elements to consider when crafting and sharing your testimony effectively.

1. Understanding the Purpose of Your Testimony

A testimony is more than just recounting events; it's about communicating lessons learned, showcasing transformation, and offering hope or guidance to others. Identifying the purpose of your testimony will help you tailor it to your audience and ensure it resonates with them. Ask yourself:

What message do I want to convey?

How can my experience benefit or inspire others?

2. Structure Your Testimony Effectively

A well-structured testimony is engaging and easy to follow. Consider using the following format:

Introduction: Briefly introduce yourself and provide context for your testimony.

Before the Change: Describe your situation or challenge, being authentic about the struggles or obstacles.

The Turning Point: Highlight the moment of realization, decision, or external help that led to change.

After the Change: Share the positive outcomes, growth, or lessons learned since the turning point.

Call to Action or Encouragement: Conclude with a message of Encouragement, advice, or an invitation for your audience to reflect on their journey.

3. Be Authentic and Vulnerable

Authenticity is key to making your testimony impactful. Share your story honestly, even the difficult parts, as this vulnerability fosters trust and relatability. Avoid embellishing or minimizing your experiences; the power of your testimony lies in its truthfulness.

4. Tailor Your Testimony to Your Audience

Consider who you speak to and adapt your tone, language, and content to suit them. For example:

Focus on lessons and strategies applicable to your field in a professional setting.

When speaking to a community or faith-based group, emphasize values, beliefs, or spiritual growth.

5. Incorporate Key Details Without Overwhelming

While providing context and specifics is important, avoid overloading your testimony with unnecessary details. Focus on the most impactful elements of your journey to maintain your audience's engagement and ensure your message is clear.

6. Highlight the Role of Gratitude and Support

Acknowledge the people, circumstances, or personal practices that supported your transformation. Gratitude for those who guided or encouraged you can make your testimony uplifting and relatable.

7. Practice Delivery

If you share your testimony verbally, practice beforehand to ensure clarity and confidence. Pay attention to your tone, pacing, and body language. A heartfelt and composed delivery can make your message more compelling.

8. Be Open to Feedback and Connection

Sharing your testimony often invites others to share their own experiences. Be prepared to listen and engage with your audience. Their feedback and stories can enrich your understanding and build meaningful connections.

9. Use Your Testimony as a Tool for Growth

Reflecting on and sharing your journey can reinforce your lessons and remind you of your progress. It also serves as a reminder of the value of resilience, gratitude, and personal growth.

Your journey is a unique and powerful story filled with lessons, growth, and triumphs. By sharing it, you can ignite hope, offer guidance, and inspire others to overcome their challenges. Everyone has a story worth telling; yours could be the beacon someone needs to navigate their path.

Why Share Your Story?

Your experiences—no matter how ordinary they may seem—hold the potential to resonate deeply with others. They can:

Empower Others: Hearing how you've navigated challenges can motivate others to tackle their own.

Foster Connection: Sharing creates a sense of community and reminds others they're not alone.

Spark Change: Your story might encourage someone to make a bold decision, leap of faith, or pursue their dreams.

Ways to Inspire Through Your Journey

Be Genuine: Authenticity resonates. Share your story honestly, highlighting both the struggles and the successes.

Focus on Lessons: Frame your experiences around what you've learned, providing insights that others can apply to their own lives.

Offer Hope: Even if your journey isn't fully complete, share how you've found strength, resilience, or positivity in the process.

Be Vulnerable: Don't shy away from sharing your fears or failures. They make your story relatable and show that even in difficult times, growth is possible.

Simple Ways to Start Inspiring Others

Write it Down: Start a blog, journal, or post on social media to share your reflections and milestones.

Speak Out: Share your journey in conversations, at events, or through podcasts.

Support Others: Offer Encouragement to those going through similar challenges. Sometimes, your lived experience can be the advice they need.

Celebrate the Small Wins: Highlighting incremental progress shows others that success is built over time.

Remember: Your Story Matters

Even if you think your experiences are too small or ordinary to share, someone else may find profound meaning in them. By opening up about your journey, you invite others to see the possibilities in their lives.

A Ripple Effect of Inspiration

Your journey inspires individuals and creates a ripple effect. The person you encourage might, in turn, inspire someone else, amplifying the impact of your story.

Take the first step. Share your journey, no matter where you are, and let it be a light for others. You can inspire, empower, and uplift—one story at a time.

Living in Joy

Joy is not a luxury—it's a necessity for a rich and meaningful life. Are you ready to invite more laughter, delight, and happiness into your days? Let's journey to uncover 100 ways to infuse your life with positivity and fulfillment. These strategies help you discover joy and sustain it in your everyday routine.

1. Cultivate Gratitude

Start each day by reflecting on the things you're grateful for. Gratitude helps you focus on life's positives and fosters a happier outlook.

2. Practice Mindfulness

Being present in the moment can reduce stress and elevate well-being. To stay centered, engage in meditation or deep-breathing exercises.

3. Build Meaningful Relationships

Nurture your connections with loved ones. Strong relationships are a cornerstone of happiness.

4. Pursue Your Passions

Engage in activities you love. Hobbies bring excitement and purpose to your life.

5. Show Yourself Compassion

Treat yourself with kindness. Accept your imperfections and commit to personal growth.

Practical Steps to a Joyful Life

- Stay Active
- Physical activity releases endorphins, boosting your mood naturally.
- Declutter Your Space
- A tidy environment fosters a calm mind. Organize your surroundings to reduce stress.
- Seek Adventure

- Explore new experiences to rekindle your sense of wonder.
- Limit Screen Time

Set boundaries on digital use to create space for meaningful interactions and activities.

Acts of Joyful Living

Volunteer: Contributing to your community instills purpose.

Connect with Nature: Time outdoors rejuvenates the spirit.

Laugh Often: Laughter is a natural stress reliever.

Practice Forgiveness: Letting go of grudges frees you to focus on happiness.

By adopting these habits, you can craft a life rich in joy and fulfillment. No matter how small, each step you take is a stride toward a more positive and meaningful existence. So dive in, explore, and let joy lead the way!

Joy as a spiritual practice.

Joy is a profound spiritual practice rooted in faith, grace, gratitude, hope, and love. It is the unadulterated delight in the gift of being alive. Joy emerges as our exuberant response to happiness, pleasurable experiences, and an awareness of life's abundance. We also experience profound fulfillment when serving others and celebrating their successes and good fortune.

You can invite joy into your life by creating moments of celebration. Host events to honor life's transitions and milestones. Pause to toast the small but significant moments of happiness that brighten your day. Dance freely and often — jump for joy! Life is not merely to be endured but embraced and enjoyed with open arms.

Why This Practice May Be for You

Joy is often paired with its emotional counterparts. We speak of joy and sorrow, happiness and sadness, smiles and tears, ecstasy and agony. Experiencing one often heightens our awareness of the other. For instance, sorrow may deepen because it follows the joy of a cherished relationship. Similarly, laughter so deep it brings tears reflects the interconnectedness of these emotions.

Joy rarely stands alone; it is part of a tapestry of feelings that enrich our lives. The key is to embrace the intensity of these emotions with gratitude. In moments of sorrow and sadness, when tears flow freely, remember they are often the precursors to joy, guiding you toward a renewed sense of delight.

Daily Cues, Reminders, Vows, and Blessings

Passing a smiling person on the street reminds me to practice joy.

Watching people dance at a party inspires me to release the joy within.

Knowing the pleasure of making others happy, I vow to practice joy.

Blessed is Lady Wisdom, who draws boundless joy from the depths of our souls.

Joy is more than a fleeting emotion; it is a deep and intentional spiritual practice rooted in faith, grace, gratitude, hope, and love. It reflects the pure delight of being alive and fully present. Joy arises when we embrace happiness, savor moments of pleasure, and recognize the abundance in our lives. It also reveals itself in the quiet fulfillment of serving others and genuinely celebrating their successes and blessings.

To cultivate joy as a spiritual practice, create space for celebration. Mark milestones and transitions with intention, and find reasons to toast the small victories in your day. Dance with abandon, laugh deeply, and let your heart leap with gratitude. Life is not meant to be merely endured—it is a gift to be cherished and enjoyed.

The Interplay of Joy and Sorrow

Joy often intertwines with other emotions, such as sorrow and sadness. These contrasts deepen our appreciation of joy, reminding us that light and shadow are part of the same experience. Sorrow, for instance, can reflect the joy we've known, such as the deep ache of losing something or someone we treasured. Laughter through tears and bittersweet moments testify to the richness of life's emotional landscape.

Embracing joy as a practice means welcoming the full spectrum of feelings, knowing that even in sorrow, joy is not far behind. Gratitude for our emotional intensity allows us to see how moments of sadness can serve as stepping stones to deeper joy.

Invitations to Practice Joy

Use everyday encounters as reminders of joy: a child's laughter, a stranger's smile, or the music rhythm that moves your soul.

Celebrate the joy of others, recognizing that their happiness adds to the collective abundance of life.

Commit to sharing joy through acts of kindness, spreading light in big and small ways.

Bless the wisdom of life, which continually draws joy from within us, even amidst challenges.

Practicing joy aligns with the divine flow of life, cultivating a spirit of gratitude and abundance that sustains us through all of life's seasons.

Reflecting on the Journey

I was too nervous to listen to the keynote. Instead, I found my room and spent hours rehearsing my speech in my head. Eventually, the room filled with attendees. The first two speakers took the stage, their words a blur as I tried to stay focused. Finally, it was my turn. I gathered my materials and made my way to the front of the room. Before I reached the podium, a familiar voice interrupted.

The woman who had called me earlier addressed the audience: "We are running late. I don't want you to miss lunch. The next speaker is not fully prepared, so feel free to leave now if you'd like."

To my dismay, the audience left—except for one man sitting in the middle of the room. Arms crossed, he said, "I'm not that hungry. Go on ahead."

At that moment, I had a choice. I could let him leave, assuming he was only staying out of pity, or I could give my absolute best effort for this one person. I chose the latter. I loaded my video, arranged my transparencies, and delivered my best presentation. When I finished, the man stood up, clapped, and handed me his card.

Unexpected Outcomes

I didn't know who he was, but his influence reached farther than I imagined. When I applied for my first job, the people reviewing my resume recognized his name. His glowing recommendation secured me a position as the AV coordinator at a psychiatric hospital, where I managed video equipment and projectors.

The Power of Reflection

Did reflecting on my journey help define my purpose? It clarified one thing: I have helped others rise above their barriers, inspiring them to act with conviction. My clients frequently feel heard, valued, and motivated to give their all.

The choices I made years ago continue to shape who I am becoming. Reflection has illuminated the worth of my experiences, adding meaning to my life—even if my purpose doesn't fit neatly into a sound bite.

Your Turn to Reflect

Think back to a pivotal moment in your own life or early career. Perhaps it was a time you overcame a challenge, made a life-changing decision, or resolved never to repeat a mistake. Ask yourself:

What prepared you for that moment?

What abilities, strengths, or energy did you discover within yourself?

How has that experience shaped the person you are today?

Now, reflect on the present:

What moments in your life today show where you make a difference?

How has that early experience influenced the way you approach your work now?

How can this reflection help you envision your next chapter?

Take time to acknowledge your journey—what you've achieved, what you've overcome, and the choices you're making now. Avoid dwelling on past regrets. Instead, celebrate your growth, resilience, and the unfolding story of your life.

Reflection Questions

Reflection: How have challenges in your life refined your character and deepened your faith? Reflect on Zechariah 13:9, where trials are compared to a refining fire.

Action: Identify a recent challenge and journal about how it shaped you positively.

Reflection: How can gratitude shift your perspective during adversity?

Your Presence Is A Gift

Action: Start a gratitude journal, listing three things you're thankful for each day, even during trials.

Reflection: Reflect on the parable of the house on the rock (Matthew 7:24-27). What foundations in your life help you stand firm during storms?

Action: Strengthen your spiritual foundation through prayer, scripture reading, or connecting with a faith community.

Reflection: What negative thoughts do you need to replace with faith-based affirmations?

Action: Create a list of affirmations grounded in faith to counteract negativity and repeat them daily.

Reflection: How can you view change as an opportunity for growth rather than a threat?

Action: Write down one area of change in your life and list three ways it could help you grow.

Chapter Eight
Living Your Gift Daily

reflecting on lessons learned.

Reflection is a powerful tool for uncovering the lessons hidden within our experiences. By looking back with intention, we gain clarity, perspective, and the opportunity to carry those insights into the future. Here's how you can guide your reflection to uncover the lessons you've learned:

1. Identify a Pivotal Moment

Think back to a time in your life that stands out—a moment of triumph, failure, or significant change. Perhaps it was an opportunity you seized, a challenge you overcame, or even a mistake that taught you a hard truth. This moment doesn't have to be grand; small experiences often yield profound insights.

Prompt: What event, decision, or interaction shaped your path meaningfully?

2. Analyze What Prepared You

Consider what equipped you to face that moment. Was it a specific skill, a mindset, or the influence of others? Perhaps your preparation came from unexpected sources, like past struggles that built resilience or relationships that offered Encouragement.

Prompt: What personal strengths, learned skills, or external influences helped you navigate that experience?

3. Discover Hidden Strengths

Often, challenging situations reveal abilities we didn't know we possessed. Maybe you demonstrated courage, creativity, or perseverance for the first time. Reflecting on these strengths deepens your self-awareness and can boost your confidence.

Prompt: What qualities or talents emerged that you hadn't recognized before?

4. Extract the Lesson

Every experience has something to teach us. It might be a new approach to problem-solving, an understanding of your values, or a better way to communicate. Focus on the key takeaway and consider how it has shaped your growth.

Prompt: What did this experience teach you about yourself, others, or the world?

5. Apply the Insight

Reflection is most valuable when it informs the present and the future. Think about how the lessons you've learned influence your decisions, relationships, or work today. Consider how you can use these insights to guide your next steps.

Prompt: How has this lesson changed how you approach challenges or opportunities?

6. Recognize Growth Over Time

Look at where you are now and trace the connection to your past experiences. Recognize your progress and how those lessons have contributed to your personal or professional success.

Prompt: How has reflecting on this moment helped you see your growth and strengths more clearly?

7. Turn Reflection into Action

Use your uncovered lessons to define your goals, refine your priorities, and inspire others. Share your story to encourage those around you to embrace their reflections and lessons.

Prompt: What action can you take today to honor what you've learned?

In today's rapidly evolving world, it's easy to lose sight of what makes us unique. Buried beneath societal expectations, self-doubt, and routine, our innate talents and gifts often go unnoticed. However, living your gift is more than just identifying your strengths—it's about embodying them fully and sharing them authentically with the world. Below are practical steps to help you discover, embrace, and live your gift with purpose and meaning.

Discovering Your Gift

1. Engage in Self-Reflection

The journey begins with understanding yourself. Reflect on these key questions:

Which activities make me lose track of time?

What skills bring me joy when I use them?

What do people frequently compliment me on?

When do I feel most alive?

2. Experiment with New Experiences

Sometimes, discovering your gift requires stepping out of your comfort zone. Try volunteering, exploring new hobbies, or enrolling in classes that spark your curiosity. Pay attention to the experiences that ignite passion within you.

3. Journal Your Insights

Dedicate a journal to exploring your gifts. Document your interests, challenges, and moments of joy. Regular reflection can reveal patterns and insights, guiding you toward greater clarity about your talents.

Embracing Your Gift

4. Embrace Imperfection

Living your gift does not mean striving for perfection. Accept that growth is a journey, and imperfections are a natural part of learning. Allow yourself the grace to improve over time.

5. Practice Mindfulness

Mindfulness helps you stay connected to your inner self and passions. Integrate meditation, yoga, or simply being present into your daily routine to focus on what truly matters.

6. Commit to Lifelong Learning

Nurture your gift by expanding your knowledge and skills. Whether through formal courses, workshops, or mentorship, continued learning strengthens your expertise and confidence.

Sharing Your Gift

7. Start Small

You don't need to make monumental changes overnight. Begin by incorporating your talents into your everyday life. Share your cooking skills with friends, write thoughtful social media posts, or contribute to your community in small but impactful ways.

8. Build a Supportive Community

Surround yourself with people who inspire and encourage you. Join groups, clubs, or online communities aligned with your interests. These connections can provide valuable insights and support as you share your gift.

9. Collaborate with Others

Collaboration allows you to amplify your impact. Partner with individuals whose skills complement your own to create something meaningful that reaches a wider audience.

Living Authentically

10. Stay True to Your Values

Avoid comparing yourself to others. Your journey is uniquely yours. Stay grounded in your values and focus on what resonates with you rather than conforming to external expectations.

11. Cultivate Gratitude

Gratitude shifts your mindset toward abundance. Appreciate the gifts you already possess and cherish the moments you can share with others.

12. Establish Boundaries

Set boundaries to protect your time and energy. Know when to say no to opportunities that do not align with your mission or drain your resources.

Overcoming Challenges

13. Tackle Self-Doubt

Self-doubt is a common obstacle. Combat it by practicing positive affirmations, surrounding yourself with supportive individuals, and reminding yourself that doubt is a normal part of the process.

14. Embrace Failure as Growth

Failure is not the end but a stepping stone to success. Each setback provides valuable lessons that can refine your skills and deepen your understanding of your gift.

15. Practice Patience

Living your gift is a journey, not a race. Progress may be gradual, but perseverance and consistency will lead to growth and fulfillment.

By taking these steps, you can uncover and live your unique gift with authenticity and purpose, enriching your life and those around you.

Everyday Presence

In today's fast-paced world, it's easy to become overwhelmed by the distractions and demands of daily life. However, embracing the power of presence can significantly enhance our well-being, deepen our relationships, and elevate our overall quality of life. This article explores the importance of cultivating presence and offers practical strategies for integrating this transformative state into everyday life.

1. What is Presence?

Presence is the art of fully immersing yourself in the present moment, free from distractions and mental clutter. It means being acutely aware of your thoughts, emotions, physical sensations, and environment. When you practice presence, you establish a profound connection with yourself, others, and the world, creating a foundation for meaningful and authentic experiences.

2. The Benefits of Presence

Developing presence can bring a wealth of benefits to your personal and emotional well-being:

Reduced Stress: Focusing on the present moment helps release concerns about the past or future, promoting a sense of calm and inner peace.

Improved Productivity: Concentrating on one task at a time can boost your focus, efficiency, and overall performance.

Deeper Relationships: Being present in interactions fosters active listening, empathy, and authentic connection, strengthening bonds with others.

Heightened Self-Awareness: Presence allows you to tune into your inner world, helping you understand your thoughts and emotions more clearly.

Increased Joy and Gratitude: Living in the moment enables you to savor life's small pleasures, fostering a sense of gratitude and happiness.

3. Practical Tips for Cultivating Presence

Incorporating presence into your daily routine doesn't have to be complicated. Here are actionable steps to get started:

Practice Mindfulness Meditation: Dedicate a few minutes daily to focus on your breath or observe your body's sensations. This practice enhances your ability to remain grounded in the present.

Engage Your Senses: Use your senses to anchor yourself in the moment. Notice the colors, sounds, scents, textures, and tastes around you.

Listen Deeply: During conversations, give the speaker your undivided attention. Approach each interaction with curiosity and empathy, avoiding distractions like phones or wandering thoughts.

Mindful Activity Engagement: Transform mundane tasks like eating, walking, or cleaning into opportunities for Mindfulness. Focus on the movements, sensations, and details of each activity.

Set Technology Boundaries: Reduce digital distractions by setting specific times to check emails or social media. Create technology-free zones or periods to encourage presence.

Prioritize Self-Care: Nurture yourself with activities that rejuvenate your mind, body, and spirit, such as exercise, journaling, spending time outdoors, or engaging in hobbies.

Cultivate Gratitude: Take moments throughout your day to appreciate your surroundings and the positives in your life. Gratitude fosters a sense of fulfillment and connection to the present.

Infuse Everyday Tasks with Mindfulness: Even simple routines, like brushing your teeth or washing dishes, can be moments of presence. Focus on the textures, movements, and sensations to remain fully engaged.

4. Everyday Presence in Action

Cultivating presence doesn't require grand gestures; it thrives in the simplicity of daily life. Whether you're savoring a cup of coffee, feeling the sun's warmth on your skin, or sharing a genuine laugh with a loved one, these moments of awareness anchor you to the here and now. Integrating Mindfulness into your routine allows you to transform ordinary experiences into opportunities for profound connection and joy.

In embracing presence, you not only navigate life's demands with greater ease but also unlock the potential for deeper fulfillment, gratitude, and connection. Start small, stay consistent, and witness the profound impact that living in the moment can have on your life.

Habits for consistently embodying one's purpose.

Consistently embodying one's purpose requires cultivating habits that align daily actions with core values and long-term goals. These habits help bridge the gap between intention and action, allowing individuals to live a life of meaning and fulfillment. Below are key habits to adopt:

1. Clarify and Reaffirm Your Purpose

Reflect on your purpose regularly through journaling or meditation. Write down your "why" and revisit it frequently to ensure it remains clear and meaningful.

Create a vision board or mantra as a visual or verbal reminder of your purpose.

2. Set Intentional Goals

Break your purpose into actionable, measurable goals that you can work toward daily. For example, if you aim to empower others, set goals like mentoring someone or sharing knowledge regularly.

Align your short-term actions with long-term aspirations to stay motivated and focused.

3. Develop a Morning Routine

Start each day with practices that center you and remind you of your purpose. These might include mindfulness exercises, reading affirmations, or planning intentional actions.

Dedicate the first moments of your morning to grounding activities that prepare you to approach the day with clarity and focus.

4. Practice Mindful Decision-Making

Before taking action, ask yourself: "Does this align with my purpose?" Making decisions with this question in mind ensures consistency with your values.

Be mindful of saying "no" to opportunities or tasks that do not serve your purpose, preserving time and energy for what truly matters.

5. Embrace Continuous Learning

Commit to lifelong learning that enhances your ability to live out your purpose. Read books, take courses, or seek mentorship in areas that support your mission.

Reflect on experiences, both successes and challenges, to refine your understanding of your purpose.

6. Surround Yourself with Purpose-Driven People

Build a community of like-minded individuals who share similar values or inspire you to stay true to your purpose.

Engage in meaningful conversations and collaborations that reinforce your commitment to your goals.

7. Practice Gratitude and Reflection

Keep a gratitude journal to recognize progress and celebrate moments that reflect your purpose.

End each day by reflecting on how your actions aligned with your purpose and identifying areas for improvement.

8. Take Care of Your Well-Being

Prioritize physical, mental, and emotional health to sustain the energy needed to pursue your purpose.

To maintain balance, incorporate self-care practices, such as regular exercise, healthy eating, and adequate rest.

9. Act with Consistency

Embed purpose-driven actions into your daily routine. Even small, consistent steps accumulate into meaningful progress over time.

Focusing on the bigger picture and the impact of your actions can help you maintain discipline, even when motivation wanes.

10. Give Back and Contribute

Look for opportunities to serve others in alignment with your purpose. Volunteering, mentoring, or sharing knowledge helps reinforce your mission while making a positive impact.

11. Adapt and Evolve

Stay flexible and open to changes in your journey. As you grow, your understanding of your purpose may deepen or shift, and adapting is key to staying authentic.

Periodically review and recalibrate your goals to ensure they align with your evolving purpose.

By adopting these habits, you can consistently embody your purpose, making it a living, breathing part of your daily existence. Over time, these practices will help you stay true to your mission and inspire others to discover and live their own.

Daily Affirmations

Integrating positive affirmations into your daily routine can be a powerful way to foster success and cultivate a proactive mindset. These affirmations serve as a tool for shifting your focus, building confidence, and motivating you to achieve your goals.

Exploring Positive Affirmations

In this discussion, we'll delve into the concept of positive affirmations, examine 417 examples tailored for various scenarios, and address common questions about their scientific basis and practical application. We'll also discover how to use them effectively, including when and where they can have the greatest impact.

Instant Boost: Watch Our Video

Want a quick uplift? Check out our video featuring 10 unexpected affirmations to brighten your day and inspire positivity.

What Are Positive Affirmations?

Positive affirmations, or self-affirmations, are empowering statements you tell yourself to nurture confidence, refocus your mind, and energize your actions. They can be spoken aloud, written, listened to, or repeated internally. Consistent use helps you realign with your core values, reshape your thought patterns, and influence behavior positively. Whether starting a new project, managing stress, or grounding yourself in the present, affirmations can offer a meaningful starting point.

Examples of Positive Affirmations

Personal Strengths:

"I've got this, and nothing can hold me back!"

"In my uniqueness, I find strength. I am enough."

"Every day, I learn. Every day, I grow."

Workplace Success:

"Today's plans are tomorrow's success."

"Collaboration fuels creativity; I thrive in teamwork."

"My value extends beyond my work; I am whole and complete."

Insights from Renowned Authors

Here are inspirational affirmations from literary greats:

"The future belongs to those who believe in the beauty of their dreams." – Eleanor Roosevelt

"Peace comes from within. Do not seek it without." – Dalai Lama

"The only way to do great work is to love what you do." – Steve Jobs

Affirmations for Specific Scenarios

Before Presentations:

"My audience is rooting for my success."

"I'm excited to share my story."

For Leaders:

"I accept responsibility."

"I help others succeed."

For Women:

"I embrace joy."

"I can transform challenges into opportunities."

For Men:

"I accept and express my emotions with an open heart."

"I am focused, driven, and ready for what's ahead."

For Relationships:

Positive affirmations reinforce mutual understanding, compassion, and communication, nurturing deeper connections.

The Science Behind Affirmations

By incorporating affirmations into your routine, you engage in cognitive restructuring, which influences neural pathways. This practice helps to replace negative thought patterns with empowering beliefs, fostering emotional resilience and a positive outlook.

Affirmations are a versatile tool for personal growth and success. These statements can guide and support you whether you seek inspiration, clarity, or a sense of purpose. With consistent use, you can reshape your mindset, build confidence, and embrace new opportunities with optimism and courage.

Affirmations rooted in Scripture.

General Encouragement

"I am fearfully and wonderfully made, and my soul knows it well." (Psalm 139:14)

"God is my refuge and strength, an ever-present help in trouble." (Psalm 46:1)

"I can do all things through Christ who strengthens me." (Philippians 4:13)

"The Lord will fight for me; I need only to be still." (Exodus 14:14)

"I am more than a conqueror through Him who loves me." (Romans 8:37)

For Overcoming Fear and Anxiety

"I will not fear, for God is with me; He strengthens me and upholds me with His righteous right hand." (Isaiah 41:10)

"The peace of God guards my heart and mind in Christ Jesus." (Philippians 4:7)

"God has not given me a spirit of fear, but of power, love, and a sound mind." (2 Timothy 1:7)

"I cast all my cares on Him because He cares for me." (1 Peter 5:7)

"I trust in the Lord with all my heart and lean not on my understanding." (Proverbs 3:5-6)

For Success and Purpose

"The Lord has plans to prosper me and not to harm me, plans to give me hope and a future." (Jeremiah 29:11)

"God's grace is sufficient for me, and His power is made perfect in my weakness." (2 Corinthians 12:9)

"I am created in Christ Jesus to do good works, which God prepared in advance for me to do." (Ephesians 2:10)

"Commit to the Lord whatever I do, and my plans will succeed." (Proverbs 16:3)

"I seek first God's kingdom and righteousness, and all I need is provided." (Matthew 6:33)

For Leadership and Influence

"I am the light of the world; I let my light shine before others." (Matthew 5:14-16)

"The Lord establishes the steps of the righteous; He delights in my way." (Psalm 37:23)

"I lead with wisdom and integrity, guided by God's Word." (Proverbs 4:7)

"I serve others with humility and love, just as Christ served." (Mark 10:45)

"Whatever I do, I work at it with all my heart as working for the Lord, not for men." (Colossians 3:23)

For Relationships

"I love because He first loved me." (1 John 4:19)

"I am patient and kind; I do not envy or boast. I keep no record of wrongs." (1 Corinthians 13:4-5)

"As far as it depends on me, I live at peace with everyone." (Romans 12:18)

"I bear with others in love, striving for unity in the Spirit." (Ephesians 4:2-3)

"I forgive as the Lord forgave me." (Colossians 3:13)

Practical Tips for Using Scripture-Based Affirmations

Choose Relevant Affirmations: Select affirmations that resonate with your current circumstances or challenges.

Speak Them Aloud: There's Proclaiming God's Word over your life has power. Speak these affirmations boldly and with faith.

Write Them Down: Keep a journal of affirmations or post them where you'll see them daily, like on your mirror or desk.

Meditate on the Scripture: Reflect on the verse behind each affirmation, allowing it to sink deeply into your heart.

Make Them a Habit: Consistency is key. Incorporate affirmations into your morning routine, prayer time, or before important moments.

By grounding your affirmations in Scripture, you invite God's truth to shape your thoughts, guide your actions, and bring His peace and joy into your life.

Walking by Faith

Walking by faith means stepping into the unknown, trusting God to guide and reveal His plans as you walk in obedience. Abraham is a powerful example of this trust; he left his homeland without knowing his destination, simply following God's call (Genesis 12:1). Similarly, walking by faith requires unwavering belief in the dreams God plants in your heart, even amid adversity, as seen in Joseph's life. Despite the betrayal, false accusations, and imprisonment, Joseph remained steadfast, trusting God's purpose (Genesis 37-50).

Faith also demands determination to follow God's will despite life's challenges. Daniel exemplifies this resolve by refusing to defile himself, choosing obedience over compromise (Daniel 1:8). Walking by faith can also mean standing boldly for others, as Esther did when she risked her life to save her people from destruction (Esther). Faith calls for courage, sacrifice, and even the willingness to appear foolish, as Noah did when building an ark in a world unfamiliar with rain, or Abraham believing he would father nations at an advanced age. It's the same faith Moses demonstrated when he declared that God would provide meat for the Israelites despite no visible means, or Joshua as he marched around Jericho's walls in obedience to God's unconventional plan.

Walking by faith requires stepping outside your comfort zone and allowing God to disrupt your carefully curated life. It means rejecting cultural norms of convenience and predictability to embrace God's transformative work. Perhaps God calls you to adopt or foster children, leave a secure job for mission work, or trade worldly comforts for eternal treasures. Sometimes, faith journeys begin with pain—through betrayal, infertility, addiction, or unimaginable loss. Yet, surrendering to God can lead to profound transformation and renewal, even in life's upheavals.

Faith doesn't shield you from trials but refines and prepares you for God's purposes. As you surrender your life, dreams, and pain to Him, God will build a faith that moves mountains and invites His divine presence. He will teach you to live with abandon, embracing His grace and fullness. In the wilderness seasons, when life feels uncertain, God's guidance—like a cloud by day and fire by night—will sustain you, leading you toward His promises.

Perhaps you feel weary, clinging to hope when others have given up. You're not alone. God is raising a remnant of believers who will obey Him at any cost, whose faith has been tested and purified through trials (James 1:2). He seeks those who believe in His abundant life (John 10:10) and cling to His promises even in hopeless circumstances. He calls you to be part of this remnant, molded and refined for His glory.

Walking by faith invites you to trust God completely, even when life seems out of control. He promises to be with you in every step, strengthening and preparing you for greater things (Ephesians 3:20-21). By trusting Him wholeheartedly (Proverbs 3:5-6) and walking daily in the Spirit (John 14:12), you become a light to a world desperately needing hope.

Wherever you are in your journey of faith, surrender to God. Let Him use your life—your struggles and victories—for His purposes. Step out of the boat, keep your eyes fixed on Jesus, and walk by faith into the extraordinary plans He has for you. It is a decision that transforms not only your life but also the lives of those around you.

Walking by faith is a profound spiritual journey that challenges believers to trust God's sovereignty and promises beyond what is visible or tangible. It's an intentional reliance on God's guidance and goodness, particularly in moments of uncertainty, trial, or decision-making. By delving into practical applications and biblical foundations, we can better understand how to deepen our faith and align our lives with God's will.

What Does It Mean to Walk by Faith?

Walking by faith transcends human understanding and control, requiring believers to trust God fully, even when the path ahead is unclear. It involves surrendering personal plans and fears to God's greater wisdom, embodying a confidence rooted in His character and promises. As Paul states in 2 Corinthians 5:7, "For we live by faith, not by sight," this journey relies not on visible evidence but on spiritual assurance and conviction.

10 Ways to Walk by Faith

Trusting God in Difficult Times

Life's challenges test our faith, but they also refine it. By clinging to God's promises of strength and peace (Isaiah 41:10), we demonstrate trust in His ability to work all things for our good (Romans 8:28).

Making Decisions Based on Conviction

Walking by faith often means choosing God's principles over worldly logic. Like Daniel, who refused to compromise his beliefs (Daniel 1:8), we are called to align our decisions with God's Word, even when difficult.

Stepping Out in Faith for Ministry

Responding to God's call—whether serving locally or internationally—requires faith that He will equip and sustain us. Abraham's journey to an unknown land (Genesis 12:1) reminds us of the blessings that follow obedience.

Relying on God for Provision

Trusting God to meet our needs, even in scarcity, reflects faith in Him as Jehovah-Jireh. Just as He provided manna for the Israelites in the wilderness (Exodus 16), He will provide for us.

Maintaining Faith in Suffering

Trials and loss can shake our faith but also deepen our dependence on God. Job's steadfast faith amidst unimaginable loss exemplifies the hope we find in God's presence during suffering (Job 1:21).

Forgiving and Loving Others

Faith in relationships means choosing forgiveness and Love, even when it feels undeserved. Jesus' command to forgive as we have been forgiven (Matthew 6:14) calls us to reflect His grace to others.

Seeking God's Kingdom First

Prioritizing God's will in decisions reflects faith in His provision. Matthew 6:33 reminds us that everything else will fall into place when we seek His kingdom first.

Practicing Gratitude in All Circumstances

Gratitude shifts our focus from challenges to God's faithfulness, even in trials. Paul's exhortation to "give thanks in all circumstances" (1 Thessalonians 5:18) highlights the transformative power of gratitude.

Sharing the Gospel Boldly

Walking by faith includes sharing our testimony and the gospel and trusting God to use our words to touch hearts (Romans 10:14-15).

Investing in Spiritual Growth

Faith grows through disciplines like prayer, Bible study, and fellowship. These practices deepen our relationship with God, allowing us to trust Him more fully.

Biblical Foundations of Walking by Faith

Hebrews 11, often called the "Hall of Faith," provides inspiring examples of walking by faith. Abraham's obedience, Moses' courage, and Noah's trust in God's instruction to build the ark (Genesis 6) all underscore the essence of faith: trusting God's promises, even when fulfillment seems impossible. Faith is "confidence in what we hope for and assurance about what we do not see" (Hebrews 11:1), reminding believers to anchor their trust in God's unseen yet unfailing faithfulness.

Encouragement for Your Faith Journey

Walking by faith can be challenging, especially when life feels uncertain or overwhelming. Yet, God's promises offer reassurance: He will never leave nor forsake us (Deuteronomy 31:6), and His plans are for our ultimate good (Jeremiah 29:11). Embrace each step of the journey, knowing that God is refining your faith and preparing you for His purposes. By surrendering to Him, you will experience His abundant life and peace (John 10:10).

Let this journey be a testament to God's glory and a beacon of hope for others. Step out in faith, trusting Him to guide, sustain, and transform you in ways beyond what you can imagine.

Giving Back

Giving back is a radiant beacon of hope and compassion in a world often dominated by self-interest and individualism. Generosity, in its many forms, holds the power to transform communities, strengthen connections, and drive meaningful Change. This exploration delves into the significance of giving back and highlights its profound impact on individuals and society.

The Essence of Generosity

What Does Giving Back Mean?

Giving back encompasses offering time, resources, or skills to benefit others or the community. Whether through volunteering, monetary donations, or sharing knowledge, giving back is rooted in selflessness and the aspiration to create positive Change. It's an intentional act of service that reflects a commitment to the well-being of others and the larger society.

Generosity Through a Biblical Lens

Scriptural teachings emphasize the importance of generosity. For instance, 2 Corinthians 9:7 (NIV) reminds us, "Each of you should give what you have decided in your heart to give, not reluctantly or under compulsion, for God loves a cheerful giver." This verse underscores the idea that true giving stems from joy and willingness rather than obligation, reflecting one's heart and character.

The Benefits of Giving Back

Strengthening Communities

Generosity builds unity by fostering collective action and support. Community service projects, charitable donations, or neighborhood improvement efforts create bonds that enhance community cohesion and resilience.

Promoting Social Justice

Giving back contributes to addressing inequality by uplifting marginalized groups. Supporting causes that advocate for the underprivileged reflects a commitment to fairness and justice. Proverbs 31:8-9 (NIV) encourages us to "Speak up for those who cannot speak for themselves, for the rights of all who are destitute." By doing so, we help create a more equitable world.

Encouraging Personal Growth

Generosity cultivates empathy and compassion, broadening one's perspective of the world. It deepens understanding, instills a sense of purpose, and promotes fulfillment, enriching the giver's journey.

Fostering Relationships

Acts of generosity often lead to meaningful and lasting relationships. Shared values of compassion and service bring people together, fostering networks of support and belonging.

Enhancing Happiness and Well-Being

Research consistently shows that giving back boosts overall happiness. Acts 20:35 (NIV) reflects this truth: "It is more blessed to give than to receive." By serving others, we experience the joy of contributing to the greater good.

Practical Ways to Give Back

Volunteering Time

Offering your time to support causes such as mentoring, community cleanups, or working at a food bank can make a tangible difference in the lives of others.

Donating to Charitable Causes

Financial contributions to organizations aligned with your values can help sustain efforts to aid those in need, enabling long-term impact.

Sharing Expertise

Using your unique skills to teach, mentor, or provide free services can empower others and drive community growth.

Engaging in Random Acts of Kindness

Simple acts of kindness, like helping a neighbor, paying for someone's coffee, or offering a compliment, can brighten days and spread positivity. Though small, these gestures echo the principles of giving back by fostering goodwill.

In a society often characterized by competition and individual pursuits, giving back not only brings people together but also enriches lives on a profound level. Whether through grand gestures or small acts, generosity enables us to connect, inspire, and build a better world.

Sharing one's gifts aligns with fulfilling divine purpose by using the talents and blessings we have received to serve others, glorify God, and contribute to the greater good. Giving reflects a selfless acknowledgment that our abilities, resources, and opportunities are not solely for personal gain but to bless others and advance God's plans for humanity.

Rooted in Divine Intent

The Bible teaches that each person is uniquely created and endowed with gifts for a specific purpose. Ephesians 2:10 (NIV) states, "For we are God's handiwork, created in Christ Jesus to do good works, which God prepared in advance for us to do." This verse emphasizes that our talents are divinely assigned, not by accident, but with intentionality, to carry out meaningful work that fulfills God's greater design.

Reflecting God's Love Through Service

When we share our gifts, we mirror God's Love and grace to others. Jesus' life serves as the ultimate example of selflessness and service. Matthew 20:28 (NIV) highlights this: "The Son of Man did not come to be served, but to serve, and to give his life as a ransom for many." In the same way, sharing our gifts enables us to reflect Christ's Love by meeting the needs of others, uplifting communities, and offering hope to those around us.

Building the Body of Christ

The Apostle Paul explains in 1 Corinthians 12:4-7 (NIV) that spiritual gifts are given to each individual to build up the collective body of Christ:

"There are different kinds of gifts, but the same Spirit distributes them. There are different kinds of service, but the same Lord. There are different kinds of working, but in all of them and everyone, it is the same God at work. The manifestation of the Spirit is given to each one for the common good."

By sharing our talents and resources, we contribute to the flourishing of the church and the broader community, fostering unity and mutual support.

Fulfilling the Command to Love

Jesus commands us to love our neighbors as ourselves (Mark 12:31). Sharing our gifts—whether through teaching, giving, serving, or creating—is a tangible expression of this Love. It allows us to address the needs of others, promote equity, and make a positive impact, all of which are integral to living out God's commandments.

Bringing Glory to God

Ultimately, using our gifts for others glorifies God by showcasing His goodness and provision. Matthew 5:16 (NIV) encourages believers: "Let your light shine before others, that they may see your good deeds and glorify your Father in heaven." Sharing what we have magnifies God's name and inspires others to recognize His presence in their lives.

Personal Fulfillment and Spiritual Growth

We find fulfillment and a deeper connection to God in serving others through our gifts. Romans 12:6-8 (NIV) reminds us to actively use our gifts: "We have different gifts, according to the grace given to each of us. If your gift is prophesying, prophesy by your faith; if it is serving, then serve; if it is teaching, then teach..." Engaging our gifts as God intended brings joy and strengthens our faith as we witness the transformative impact of His work through us.

We participate in a divine purpose, transcending personal achievements by sharing our gifts. Through this selfless act, we fulfill God's calling, demonstrate His Love, and contribute to unfolding His kingdom on earth.

Staying Aligned Through Seasons

Living in harmony with the seasons allows us to reconnect with nature's rhythms, fostering well-being and a deeper connection to the world. Here are simple, actionable ways to embrace a seasonal lifestyle:

1. Observe the Changing Seasons

Take time each day to notice the subtle changes as seasons shift. Spend a few moments outdoors at the same time daily, paying attention to the sights, sounds, and sensations around you. You could even keep a journal to document these observations, noting patterns and transformations over time.

As each season begins, consider how you might honor its arrival. Simple rituals like planting spring flowers or displaying a bowl of gourds in the fall can help you feel more in tune with nature's cycles.

2. Eat Seasonally

Eating seasonally aligns your diet with nature's rhythms, benefiting your body and the environment. Seasonal foods are harvested at their peak, offering maximum flavor and nutritional value.

Local Seasonal Choices: Incorporate foods that grow naturally in your area during each season. For instance, enjoy butternut squash in the fall, citrus fruits in winter, strawberries in spring, and watermelon in summer.

Environmental Impact: By choosing local, seasonal produce, you reduce the carbon footprint of transporting out-of-season fruits and vegetables from distant locations.

Supporting Local Farmers: Shopping at farmer's markets is an excellent way to discover what's in season while supporting local agriculture and businesses.

Not sure what's in season? Farmer's markets or local produce guides are excellent resources.

3. Supplement Seasonally

As seasons change, certain nutrients may become less accessible through fresh produce. Supplements can help bridge the gap:

Consider a vitamin C supplement in summer if fresh citrus isn't readily available.

You might need extra iron in winter if leafy greens like spinach are out of season.

Incorporate year-round supplements like Just Thrive, which supports gut health and boosts immunity, ensuring your body benefits from seasonal nutrition all year.

By observing the world around you and making conscious choices about how you eat and live, you can foster a lifestyle that is not only more sustainable but also deeply rewarding. Living seasonally is a journey of reconnecting with nature, appreciating its bounty, and cultivating a life balanced with its cycles.

Adaptability and trust in every life season.

Life is a series of evolving seasons, each marked by unique opportunities, challenges, and lessons. Embracing adaptability and trust allows us to navigate these transitions with grace and resilience, fostering personal growth and fulfillment.

The Power of Adaptability

Adaptability is the ability to adjust to changing circumstances as nature adapts to seasonal shifts. It empowers us to face life's uncertainties with flexibility and openness.

Navigating Change: Whether joyful or challenging, each season of life requires us to recalibrate our expectations and strategies. For example, stepping into a new career might necessitate learning new skills, just as adjusting to parenthood demands a shift in priorities.

Cultivating Resilience: Being adaptable strengthens our capacity to recover from setbacks, helping us view challenges as opportunities for growth. This mindset allows us to thrive, even in unexpected Change.

Trusting the Process

Trust involves believing in the inherent value of every life season, even when its purpose isn't immediately clear. Trusting the process requires surrendering to the flow of life and being confident that each phase contributes to our overall journey.

Patience in Growth: Just as seeds sprout, some life seasons involve waiting and preparation. Trusting this process helps us stay grounded, knowing that progress often unfolds in time.

Faith in Challenges: Difficult seasons can feel overwhelming, yet they often bring profound transformation. Trusting in their purpose allows us to find meaning in adversity, guiding us toward inner strength and wisdom.

Adaptability and Trust in Harmony

When combined, adaptability and trust form a powerful synergy that equips us to embrace life's seasons fully:

Embracing New Beginnings: Trusting that Change is necessary and adapting to new circumstances allows us to seize fresh opportunities enthusiastically.

Letting Go: Some seasons call for releasing what no longer serves us. Trusting the wisdom of letting go while adapting to a new normal fosters emotional and spiritual growth.

Thriving in Uncertainty: Life's unpredictability is inevitable, but a balance of adaptability and trust enables us to face it with courage and optimism.

Lessons from Nature

Nature is a profound teacher of adaptability and trust. Trees shed their leaves in autumn, trusting new growth will follow in spring. Rivers adjust their course over time, flowing around obstacles while maintaining their purpose. These examples remind us that life's seasons are temporary, each preparing us for what lies ahead.

By cultivating adaptability and trust, we can navigate every life season with resilience and grace, fully embracing the beauty and wisdom that each phase brings.

Reflection Questions

How do I consistently align my daily habits with my purpose? What simple routines can I adopt to embody this alignment more fully?

What affirmations, rooted in Scripture, can I speak over myself daily to reinforce my faith and purpose?

In what areas of my life can I walk more boldly by faith, trusting God's guidance in my decisions?

How can I use my unique gifts to give back and contribute to others, fulfilling my divine purpose?

Am I staying aligned with my purpose during different life seasons? How can I embrace adaptability and trust in God's plan through change?

Chapter Nine
Leaving a Legacy

Our careers often define how we contribute to the world, allowing us to create a lasting impact through meaningful work. When driven by a deeper sense of purpose beyond financial gain, we connect with a profound sense of fulfillment that extends our influence beyond ourselves.

Starting a business or nonprofit appeals to some, but everyone can strive to build something enduring, whether working independently or within an organization. The following ideas can help you shape a legacy that lasts.

Building a Professional Legacy

1. Mentor Future Leaders

Mentorship is a powerful way to influence the next generation of professionals. Sharing your experiences, values, and guidance with aspiring leaders in your field allows you to "pay it forward." Discuss your journey, address their concerns, and inspire them to create impactful careers.

2. Share Your Expertise

Capture the knowledge and insights you've gained throughout your career. Consider contributing to trade publications, authoring a book, or maintaining a blog. Online platforms provide cost-effective ways to share your expertise, ensuring that your wisdom continues to inspire and educate even in retirement.

3. Stay Engaged Post-Retirement

Remaining connected to your professional community after retirement ensures your legacy continues to grow. Act as a resource, mentor, or consultant, and nurture relationships with former colleagues and clients. Staying active also contributes to a longer and more fulfilling retirement.

Preserving a Legacy for Your Family

4. Document Life in Your Era

Recording your experiences and perspectives on current events provides a unique gift for future generations. Writing letters or journaling significant milestones allows your descendants to connect with history through your lens.

5. Curate Your Family's History

Act as your family's historian by compiling photos, heirlooms, or documents. Create timelines that align personal stories with major world events or undertake genealogical research. This effort preserves your family's narrative for generations.

6. Share Your Life Story

Writing your memoir or autobiography allows you to pass down lessons and memories. Sharing your life's journey enriches your family's legacy and preserves your unique story.

7. Record Audio or Video Memories

For those who find speaking easier than writing, creating audio or video recordings can be a meaningful way to document family stories. Use these platforms to narrate old photographs, share interviews, or offer personal insights that family members can cherish for years Contributing to the Broader World

8. Raise the Next Generation Well

One of the most impactful ways to leave a legacy is by nurturing responsible, kind, and capable children. Instilling positive values in them shapes their futures and the communities they influence.

9. Volunteer for Causes You Value

Volunteering allows you to actively contribute to society. Dedicate your time and skills to organizations that align with your passions. The impact of your efforts will resonate throughout your community and beyond.

10. Share Life Lessons

A legacy letter is a personal and timeless way to pass on wisdom. Share the values, experiences, and lessons that have shaped your life, leaving a guiding light for loved ones to follow.

11. Practice and Teach Love

Meeting hatred with Love is a transformative act. Teaching compassion and understanding fosters a more peaceful society and strengthens humanity's ability to thrive together.

12. Take Initiative to Create Change

Seize opportunities to improve your community. Whether starting a local program, advocating for Change, or spearheading initiatives like community gardens or literacy campaigns, your actions can create a legacy of positive impact.

By intentionally shaping your professional and personal contributions, you can leave a legacy that resonates across generations—an enduring testament to a life well-lived.

Legacy of Faith

What if you could pass on a legacy to your family that surpasses material wealth, empowering them to overcome sickness, achieve financial stability, and thrive in meaningful relationships? This would be a legacy of unwavering faith that moves mountains, defeats challenges, and stands firm in every storm.

Billy Graham once said, "The greatest legacy one can pass on to one's children and grandchildren is a legacy of character and faith." You, too, can create and live a legacy of faith, inspiring those around you and leaving a mark on future generations. The only requirement is a commitment to being a born-again child of God. Your background, education, financial situation, or current circumstances are irrelevant. Your legacy is shaped by the choices you make today.

You don't have to wait for eternity to leave a legacy. It begins now. Here's how you can start living a legacy of faith:

1. Start Fresh, If Necessary

"Let each generation tell its children of your mighty acts." – Psalm 145:5

Even if your family history lacks a foundation of faith, you can be the one to establish it. Jeremy Pearsons, Kenneth Copeland's grandson, reminds us, "The life you live is the legacy you leave." A legacy of faith is not reserved for those with a history of religious upbringing; it's for anyone who chooses to believe in Jesus Christ. No matter your past—whether marked by brokenness, abuse, or a lack of faith—you can start anew and create a legacy that transforms your family's future.

2. Step Into Your Unique Calling

"Go from your country, your people, and your father's household…. I will make your name great." – Genesis 12:1-2 (NIV)

Faith requires individuality. While you may inherit a legacy of faith, God has a unique purpose for your life. Listen for His direction, and if He calls you to step away from your family's traditions or legacy, trust Him as Abraham did. Similarly, if your legacy includes breaking free from cycles of poverty, sickness, or negativity, rely on God's strength to build a new foundation.

3. Cultivate a Personal Relationship with God

"O God, you are my God." – Psalm 63:1 (ESV)

A true legacy of faith begins with making God your own. Your faith cannot depend solely on your parents, pastors, or others. It must be rooted in your personal experiences, miracles, and testimonies. Develop a daily relationship with Him, trust Him in all things, and let His guidance shape your path.

4. Find Your Faith Family

"Those who are planted in the house of the Lord shall flourish in the courts of our God." – Psalm 92:13 (NKJV)

A church family is a vital part of your legacy. Being part of a faith community provides support, encouragement, and an opportunity to contribute to others' lives. Even if past experiences have left you wary, remember that isolation isn't God's design. Find a church home where you can both give and receive.

5. Build Your Life on the Word of God

"Everyone then who hears these words of mine and does them will be like a wise man who built his house on the rock." – Matthew 7:24 (ESV)

A legacy of faith requires living in alignment with God's Word. This means choosing His truth over societal norms, speaking life in the face of negativity, and standing firm on biblical principles, even when challenging. Your unwavering commitment will inspire those around you.

6. Share Your Testimony

"One generation shall praise Your works to another, and shall declare Your mighty acts." – Psalm 145:4 (NKJV)

Your victories through faith are powerful tools for teaching and inspiring others. Share your stories of God's goodness with your family regularly. These moments of reflection and storytelling can plant seeds of faith that will grow in the hearts of future generations.

7. Keep Moving Forward

"I would have lost heart unless I had believed that I would see the goodness of the Lord." – Psalm 27:13 (NKJV)

Living a legacy of faith is a journey. There will be challenges, but the key is to keep walking forward, trusting in God's plan. As Gloria Copeland says, "Just keep walking." Each step you take in obedience strengthens your faith and legacy.

8. Never Give Up

"So, let's not get tired of doing what is good. At just the right time, we will reap a harvest of blessing if we don't give up." – Galatians 6:9

Perseverance is crucial. Giving up leaves no legacy. By pressing on through trials, you demonstrate the power of steadfast faith to your children and others.

By embracing these principles, you can live a legacy of faith that blesses not only your family but also the lives of countless others. Start today—your future and theirs depend on it.

Reflection Questions

What aspects of your personal or professional life align with the legacy you want to leave behind?

How can you start incorporating mentorship, shared knowledge, or family storytelling into your daily life?

Are there areas in your life where you can practice more compassion, faith, or community involvement to strengthen your impact?

How do you define a meaningful legacy in your career, family, and community?

What steps can you take today to ensure your values and lessons are passed on effectively?

In what ways can your faith or beliefs guide the legacy you aim to create?

Conclusion
Claiming

In a world that often prioritizes doing over being, it is essential to recognize the profound power of your presence. Your existence alone carries value, bringing unique energy, insights, and compassion to every interaction and space you enter. By claiming your presence, you acknowledge that your worth is not tied solely to achievements or external validation but to the authentic essence of you.

When you embrace your presence as a gift, you empower yourself to show up fully, authentically, and unapologetically. This not only enriches your own life but also inspires those around you to do the same. Through this intentional recognition of your inherent value, you create deeper connections, foster meaningful experiences, and leave an indelible impact on the world.

So, step into each moment with the awareness that your presence matters. Let your light shine, your voice be heard, and your essence be felt. By doing so, you claim the truth that you are, and always have been, a gift to this world.

Making Claiming a Daily Practice

Claiming your presence as a gift is not a one-time realization but an ongoing practice that requires intention and mindfulness. Incorporating daily habits that affirm your worth and embrace your authentic self can help anchor this truth in your life. Here are some practical steps to make claiming your presence a daily practice:

Start with Self-Affirmation

Begin each day with affirmations that remind you of your value and uniqueness. Simple phrases like "I am enough," "My presence matters," or "I bring light to the world" can set a positive tone and reinforce your inner confidence.

Practice Mindfulness

Take moments throughout the day to pause and ground yourself in the present moment. Whether through deep breaths, meditation, or a quiet reflection, mindfulness helps you reconnect with your inner self and strengthens your awareness of your presence.

Engage Authentically

Approach every interaction with authenticity and openness. Share your thoughts, emotions, and energy sincerely, and resist shrinking yourself to fit others' expectations.

Acknowledge Your Impact

Reflect on how your presence has positively influenced others, whether through a kind word, a listening ear or simply being there. Keeping a journal of these moments can remind you of your ongoing contribution to the world.

Celebrate Small Wins

Take time to celebrate the small victories and the progress you make in showing up fully each day. These celebrations reinforce the belief that you are worthy and that your presence is a gift.

Set Intentions

At the start of each day, set an intention to fully claim your space in the world. Whether speaking up in a meeting, offering kindness to someone, or simply being present, your intention can guide your actions meaningfully.

Integrating these practices into your daily routine makes claiming your presence a way of life. Over time, this intentionality will cultivate deeper self-awareness, confidence, and a sense of purpose, reminding you that your presence is a gift to be embraced and shared daily.

Other Books By The Author

Tangled Hearts

Silent Vision

Silent Vision 2 Code Name Echo

Silent Vision 3 Ghost Hunter

Man Up

Woman Up

Couple Up

Marriage is it worth the fight

Sheltered Hearts

WYGDN what you gonna do now

Empowering the Future

Artificial Love

Beyond Loss

NEXT (Negative Evaluation and Xchange Trade)

Ungrateful

The Mind

Ungrateful

License to Sin

Your Presence is a gift: Claim it.

www.ingramcontent.com/pod-product-compliance
Lightning Source LLC
LaVergne TN
LVHW050852200726
843508LV00011B/2000